'By attending to messages, gestures, signals in the surrounding streets, by inviting neighbours' stories and explanations, Attlee has assembled a searching portrait of the time of Covid.'

Marina Warner

'Full of warmth, wit and eloquence, and a rare, refreshing combination of modesty and conviction. I loved the careful anthropological questioning of the complex world on our doorsteps.'

Alexandra Harris

PRAISE FOR ATTLEE'S *ISOLARION*

'Unique and very special. Residents of East Oxford can be proud to have this eccentric advocate and eloquent explorer in their midst.'

Geoff Dyer, *The Guardian*

'A new Oxford that no guidebook has yet captured.'

Richard B. Woodward, *New York Times*

'Attlee's reading is deep and wide and engagingly circuitous, and this book frequently provides the delights of discovery that make any adventure worth undertaking.'

Rebecca Mead, *Bookforum*

'With an eclecticism that ropes in Robert Burton's *The Anatomy of Melancholy*, Foucault, a porn shop and a Jamaican restaurant, Attlee scrutinises a sense of place. He reminds me of the old scholars, chock full of intellectual curiosity and an almost alchemical sensibility.'

Ray Mattinson, Blackwell's, Oxford

PRAISE FOR ATTLEE'S *NOCTURNE*

'I know that I am going to keep this book by me for rereading.'

Diana Athill

James
Attlee

Under
the
Rainbow

Voices from
Lockdown

SHEFFIELD – LONDON – NEW YORK

First published in 2021 by And Other Stories
Sheffield – London – New York
www.andotherstories.org

For the acknowledgement of quotations, see the Acknowledgements page.

All photographs © James Attlee, apart from *Red Flags* © Alex Noble and *Grow Chives,
Save Lives* © Charlotte Attlee.

9 8 7 6 5 4 3 2 1

ISBN: 9781913505066
eBook ISBN: 9781913505073

Editor: Stefan Tobler; Copy-editor: Robina Pelham Burn; Proofreader: Sarah Terry;
Typeset in Linotype Neue Swift and Verlag by Tetragon, London; Cover Design: Steve
Leard; Printed and bound on acid-free, age-resistant Munken Premium by CPI Limited,
Croydon, UK.

And Other Stories gratefully acknowledge that our work is supported using public
funding by Arts Council England.

Under
the
Rainbow

CONTENTS

AN INTRODUCTION OF SORTS

July turns into August with no break in the humid nights and blue-skied days, creating a growing sense that this summer will last forever and that time, like much else, has stuttered to a halt. We wake each morning to the same faces and the knowledge that whatever we learn today will in all likelihood be contradicted tomorrow. Scientists and politicians appear equally confused; the only advice they agree on comes in the form of homilies that might have been delivered by our parents or grandparents: Wash your hands. Stay in and do your homework. Don't kiss strangers. Turn down the invitation to that dodgy party. As is traditional, this advice will be ignored by the young and the desperate.

Then, in the second week of the month, something shifts in the heavens and the torpor is broken. The air crackles with electricity. Drops of rain fall as you cycle in bright sunshine along the towpath by the canal, your back drenched with sweat. Someone is moving heavy furniture overhead; the sound echoes in the streets. Arriving home, you drag your partner away from yet another Zoom meeting to stand outside the back door as lightning flickers and the downpour starts. You take off your shirts and lift your arms, luxuriate. And then it's over. Water pools on the ground. The air, you both notice, smells of gunpowder.

Something has altered, it's clear. You observe people sitting in their cars in a traffic jam with the dispassionate interest of a visitor to a safari park. Do they really leave their engines running like that, so the fumes creep under people's front doors and into their lungs – is that really how it's done? It seems quaint, unbelievable. You resist the urge to tap on the windows of these stationary travellers and ask them to desist. In a few weeks, the radio announces, children will be going back to school, giving their parents more time to look for new jobs. For now, parents concentrate on booking holidays and then unbooking them as borders shift from national to viral; yet the sky is once again cross-hatched with vapour trails that must, for those who choose to follow, lead somewhere.

You'd think we'd remember when it all started; yet politicians disagree on the date when the first lockdown began, the prime minister maintaining it was 23 March 2020, the health secretary insisting it was the sixteenth. What is clear is that around the time of the spring equinox, when days were growing longer and all our instincts made us want to be together and outdoors, we were forced instead to turn inwards. By midsummer the restrictions eased a little, but by the autumn equinox, when the tilt of the earth meant the northern and southern hemispheres briefly shared equal amounts of light, figures of new infections were surging once more.

This book exists in the space between those two equinoxes, points that in the calendar signify a beginning and the beginning of an ending; events marked in the heavens by geomagnetic storms and the spectacular unfurling of the Northern Lights, while the realms below flipped between panic and stasis as time turned elastic, one hour passing in a heartbeat, the next crawling snail-like towards eternity. Beginning with an investigation of the artworks that appeared in windows over this period, led by the words of people who made them, it moves through and beyond them to the symbols, histories and causes that became points of contention during lockdown.

A moment is passing, slipping through our fingers. Was it all a dream, you wonder. Did the world of man really fall silent so that every day at 4 p.m. you'd hear the song of a blackbird high in a tree on the other side of the road, so piercingly sweet it penetrated your front door? For many, the natural world became suddenly hyperreal. Bumblebees fumbled their way into flowers, swifts screamed and flies danced, unaware they had become swooned-over social media stars. Meanwhile we were confined to our homes, forced to share the same space almost twenty-four hours a day, emerging only to jostle and squabble over essential supplies in supermarkets, or to stand outside our doors applauding, overwhelmed by a love both sudden and temporary for those who have dedicated their lives to caring for us all along.

How quickly we forget. Yet for now traces remain around us, in windows and over doorways – expressions of solidarity, hope, revolutionary fervour. They will not survive much longer: the sun causes hand-coloured rainbows and political slogans alike to fade; children outgrow their artistic efforts, demanding they be taken down.

We missed the chance to interview those who decorated the walls of caves millennia ago and the meaning of their work has slipped from our collective memory. Those who adorned their dwellings during lockdown also represent the psyche of the tribe; their fragile creations hold something of what we learnt during the months the machine was put on pause. Time now to capture their voices and their images before they are lost in the shudders and groans of a world coming back to life.

I

ARCOBALENO

Where did they come from, all those rainbows?

First sighted in windows in Italy as the country succumbed to the crisis ahead of the rest of Europe, coupled with the slogan 'Andrà tutto bene' – 'everything's going to be all right' – they spread to Spain and from there to the UK, in step with the pandemic: talismans raised against an infection that at the same time mirrored its transmission.

Bella Italia – you have given us so much. The food, the wine, the art, the music, and now rainbows in our hour of need. As if one Italian rainbow had grown so big, expanded by all the defiant Italian optimism it contained, that it shattered into thousands of smaller rainbows, their reflections caught in the windows that surveyed our empty streets. But if we want to decode their meaning it is worth remembering Italy is not only the home of Dante and Ferrante, pizza and fashionista: it is also the power centre of the Catholic world. With that in mind, 'Andrà tutto bene' reads as a three-word summary of the story of another catastrophe, that of Noah's flood, which began with a holocaust and ended with a candy-coloured arch – an arcobaleno – in the sky.

In the sixth chapter of the book of Genesis, Noah is told: 'I am going to bring floodwaters on the earth to destroy all life under the heavens, every creature that has the breath of life in it. Everything on earth will perish.' To escape the same fate, the virtuous patriarch must enter the ark along with his family, representatives of the animal kingdom and a store of food sufficient for them all.

'Then,' the Bible says, 'the Lord God shut him in.'

Divinely sanctioned lockdown. As it was in the beginning, is now, and, it sometimes feels as the months drag on, ever shall be. Each dwelling becomes an ark, bobbing on a sea of uncertainty and fear, under a rainbow flag. House windows beam their homespun messages out to the world in much the same way Noah sent out a raven and a dove, looking for dry land.

The eventual retreat of floodwaters in the Jewish and Christian scriptures was accompanied by the world's first rainbow, both a promise and a kind of note-to-self, posted on the sky. 'Whenever the rainbow appears in the clouds,' God tells Noah, 'I will see it and remember the everlasting covenant between God and all living creatures of every kind on the earth.'

The message of that rainbow, then, was clear: no more destruction of every living thing, and that's a promise. The signs that have surrounded us these past months are more ambiguous. In each country their meanings shift to accommodate local culture. When it first appears in Britain, the rainbow carries the same simple positive message as its Italian cousin. Alice Aske from Somerset sets up a Chase the Rainbow Facebook group encouraging people to tape handmade rainbows in their windows so families can spot them as they take their permitted one hour's exercise; within twenty-four hours it has 65,000 followers. The activity, the *Sun* reports on 20 March, the day the nation's schools are shut down for the first time in post-war years, is intended to 'lift spirits in the coronavirus crisis'. Elsewhere, the same day, it reports that the official number of UK cases of the virus stands at 3,269, the death toll at 184. These numbers, touchingly low from the perspective of the present, will unscroll over the coming months as a daily litany of destruction, our response shifting from curiosity to unease to horror to numbness as the toll rises by tens of thousands, exceeding that of any other European nation.

But it is only a matter of days before the feelgood rainbow begins to morph, merging with another potent totem for residents of the UK: the National Health Service. A rainbow in the window no longer merely says 'Hello! Wave! I am Alive', but instead becomes an expression of solidarity with the health workers who are putting their lives at risk treating Covid-19 patients. How and when this shift occurs is not clear – I hope to find out – but it is taken up by the public, the media and the government with enthusiasm.

We're past midsummer, allowed out of our houses once more. It's time to knock on some doors. I get on my bike and head for a nearby housing estate built of red brick in the 1920s, largely to house the families of workers in the local car assembly plant.

A man lowers the electric trimmer he is using to sculpt the already neat hedge in front of his house in order to respond to my questions. A large, neatly executed rainbow emblazoned with the three letters 'NHS' occupies a first-floor window of his property.

We've discovered that the lowest paid are the ones that we're relying on and we're still ignoring them, aren't we, he says.

You can sit in an office and get paid far more than someone who's doing a worthwhile job – that's usually the way, isn't it?

He shakes his head, slowly, struck by another thought.

There was that euphoria at the start about how kind everybody was, wasn't there?

(I have a premonition he is going to tell me it was misplaced.) But it's just that the bad 'uns aren't out and about at the moment, are they, the people that abuse things, so you're only getting the kind-hearted people. They're there all the time, but it's like everything in life, those who shout and moan the loudest will get heard and the people who just get on with it are sort of buried underneath, beavering away trying to do good.

His neighbour has certainly been doing just that. An older resident, perhaps in her seventies, she responded to the crisis with determination and energy. A Union Jack hangs from her first-floor window and a rainbow spans the net curtains downstairs. A notice is tied to her front gate, which is located at the junction of two roads.

FREE FACE MASKS

Any Donations if offered will
be gratefully accepted for the
Community Assoc.

Thank You. Stay Safe.

She found the instructions on how to make the masks on YouTube, she tells me. She's made and given away around two thousand, so far. Beavering away, in her neighbour's words. She's going to stop doing it soon; masks are easier to come by nowadays, but to start with –

Our conversation is interrupted by the arrival of family. But it's true; this woman played an important role at the beginning of the crisis. A front-line worker I know got her first face masks at this gate on her way to her job, which she was still going to, despite the lack of any protection, while the rest of the world shut down. I wander down the shorter street that leads from the gate to the park. A cul-de-sac, it is particularly rich in window art: as well as rainbows, I see an animal frieze, a Black Lives Matter poster, an entire window devoted to Extinction Rebellion. Conversations interrupted, continued in sign language. I will return.

Back on the bike, up the hill that always gets the heart going, slow down on a street of Edwardian terraces. I knock on a door next to a window decorated with a hand-drawn rainbow. It is opened by a woman, a girl of five or six peering out from behind her. I ask who did the picture, and why.

My daughter,

the woman says.

Then, to the girl, do you want to tell the man why you did it?

The girl picks up her mother's dress and hides her face in it.

– Because you told me to,

she says, her voice muffled.

This, it turns out, is a recurrent theme. A serious-faced man opens a door a little further along: his children are there somewhere in the background, but they are not invited to join our conversation. Why did his family create the artwork in their window?

It was a way of being able to express support to health workers and also an activity that got the children involved, stopped them getting bored,

he tells me.

So partly it was for something to do but also so the children would understand the impact of the crisis, appreciate what the health workers are doing, have a sense of what's at stake.

17

No danger that education is on hold in this house during lockdown. The rainbow artworks suddenly feel less spontaneous, more a task that has been set.

I move on, through sun-baked streets I know would have been decorated with artworks two months ago but are now a gallery scrubbed clean. Builders are busy on scaffolding, fixing roofs, giving houses a post-pandemic paint job, their conversations providing a quasi-divine commentary from above, gruff cherubim in a Renaissance painting.

I have developed a cycling technique that involves pedalling slowly while moving my head from side to side to scan each property from behind dark glasses. It provokes some suspicious looks, for understandable reasons.

My route is randomly generated, taking turns at corners as they issue an invitation, pausing to take photographs when doing so won't cause alarm. Taking a picture of the front window of someone's house could be considered a little intrusive – but the images are put there to be seen and today nothing is really seen until it is stored in our phone, so they cannot reasonably object, or at least this is what I tell myself. That is until I step into position in front of one such window and a woman runs from the alley alongside the house saying, hey, hey, what are you doing? What's your name? I've got children to think of . . . And I am reminded of the paedophile convictions that have made local news in recent months.

It is always a worthwhile ambition to get through a project without being punched.

I am scouring the streets of a small housing estate devoid of decoration until I spot a window of a bungalow completely blocked out with a frieze of photographs of the royal family. I can't ascertain whether these icons have been deployed to deflect the virus or merely to express an unquestioning feudal loyalty. I decide to step over a low fence for a closer look, but desist when I notice a small, elderly woman approaching me at speed. Without preamble we are deep in conversation. She is, she says, just going out shopping, but there's no telling what the weather will do. Had I seen that heavy shower yesterday? She'd just put her washing out. Oh dear, I say, and without further prompting she begins to talk about the way it's been the past few months. This lockdown has made people round here peculiar, she says. Some of them have even put up Christmas trees in their houses, to make themselves feel better.

This is a new one on me, but it has a certain logic; cut adrift from the chronological march of time, trapped in a seemingly eternal summer, perhaps forced to isolate at home with young children, why not declare it Christmas? It wouldn't surprise me if the government got behind the initiative to boost the economy, or if the front pages bore a picture of our prime minister dressed as Santa Claus. (I wasn't to know that a month or so later a backbench MP would warn the prime minister that he risked being seen as The Grinch if social distancing measures weren't lifted by Christmas – furthering the descent of a certain branch of political rhetoric into infantilism.)

Have you seen that tree round there?

the woman asks me.

There's a tree round there, as you're going to the shop? It's got NHS and Christmas baubles on it and that. If my auntie was here – she done that in Wood Farm. Because when she lived in Wood Farm the council come along and put in these little trees, now they're great big trees, but she went out and put some balls on the little tiny fir trees at Christmas! But my aunt passed away a couple of years now. She was a bit comical like that.

I commiserate about the loss of her aunt, thank her for the tip and take off. And there it is, standing in a flower bed outside a newish house at the edge of the estate, a monkey puzzle tree that's been hung with red, silver and gold baubles and little handmade notices covered in plastic. Other notices are strung along a line woven in and out of the railings. The tree, in all its spiny, prehistoric majesty, is almost as tall as the house. There is a rainbow in the window next to the front door. I ring the bell and it opens to reveal an energetic older woman holding a young child, who wriggles off her hip and comes outside, along with a dog. I compliment her on the tree and she laughs good-naturedly.

We've got 'National Health We Love You' up here,

she says, pointing to one of the notices,

but it's faded a little bit. I still keep refreshing it every so often. There's lots still going on; the National Health doesn't stop, does it? The nurses and health workers and the doctors, we need 'em, don't we? The disease hasn't gone away, that's why we're all wearing masks and very cautious and everything, but hopefully if it comes back again maybe they'll know a bit more.

She works, she tells me, as a driver for the NHS, covering hundreds of miles collecting and delivering samples and bloods throughout the county. Was she trying to make her tree look like a Christmas tree, I ask her. She laughs.

That's me, I love Christmas – I'm the Christmas bod, I'm afraid. I have got a lot of grandchildren . . . I often thought about making it like a Christmas tree but it's such a spiteful tree – a monkey tree – you can't touch it, it just gets you. We keep cutting the arms off that go out past the fence because anybody walking past will probably sue us! And I don't trust people, to be honest with you,

she continues,

if I put fairy lights out there they'd probably be gone. But these balls, they were extra balls, so I thought they can go there. The wind was knocking them onto the floor and breaking them. I don't think people took them, you'd have a job to get them off. We'll have to cut them off one day, I think. And the signs I just made willy-nilly. I did think about refreshing them because the rain gets into them. I still might keep going on it!

Who made the rainbow in your window?

That was me, everything was me – we've got pictures from the grandchildren indoors, they've done their bit, but I'm a bit OCD probably!

Back down the hill, enjoying the blessings of gravity and cool air, motion without effort always like an unearned gift. Another street, another door, three rainbows in the window. An elderly man opens at my ring, seems unsurprised by the arrival on his doorstep of a stranger with a notebook asking questions but decides to call his wife, who is better at people's names. Perhaps in her late eighties, she is sharp as a razor, the pandemic only one of many storms she has weathered.

There are three little girls who live across the road, she tells me,

they're so beautiful, and they did my rainbows – and I think they're very pleased they did them, because they bring their friends to admire our windows.

What does the rainbow mean to her, I ask.

Support for the National Health Service was what I understood. I had some reservations about it. We went out on Thursday evenings to clap – it was almost as if there was a government conspiracy, to make us clap instead of pay them a proper wage, you know . . . This idea that we've got the most wonderful National Health Service and meanwhile we're going to get Serco to run most of it – but I didn't want to be ungracious, despite my reservations. I did hear that some health workers liked it, and if they felt appreciated, of course we should do it. There was something dramatically brave about their work at the beginning when there was no PPE, no protective clothing for them – that was really brave.

I notice that as well as rainbows the couple are displaying a plain green card in their window; in fact, there is one in nearly all the windows in this street, including those that are otherwise undecorated. What does it mean, I ask the woman I've been talking to.

The green notice shows that you're still alive – it means we don't need anything, thank you very much,

she explains.

We didn't need help because we've got family nearby. It was instigated by a man who lives across the road. He does a weekly newsletter and he also organises a weekly musical event; he plays a very neat saxophone himself and we have a singsong around him in the street on a Tuesday. It went on for many weeks and months but petered out with people going away for the holidays.

It sounds like you've got a well-organised and supportive street, I say.

It's very pleasant, very pleasant,

she says ruminatively, a faraway expression on her face.

II

LOST CITY

The woman behind the triple rainbow window is not alone in her misgivings about clapping for the NHS – I hear them expressed again and again. In the first social event I have attended for a while, in early September, I have lunch with a friend I haven't seen since before the lockdown. We sit at a zinc table outside our favourite falafel bar, the one owned by a man from a city once known as the Venice of the Middle East, destroyed in a crisis of a different kind. I ask him whether there are still many decorated windows in the street he lives in.

No,

he says,

something has shifted and most of them have gone. I think it felt to people like time to take stuff down because they felt oh, actually we've been used! Our desire to express solidarity with the NHS has been manipulated by the government – by an organisation that manifestly doesn't care – and this was a ruse either to distract us from other stuff or to engage public sentiment rather than let us take political action. And at that point I think people felt the public space was no longer a place for activism, so they took stuff down.

Not everyone shares his view. A social worker who works in the city felt much more positive about the impact of the window campaign.

Families I work with told me they felt very proud that we were a country that has this wonderful NHS,

she says.

Everybody knows a nurse or a theatre technician or a hospital porter – a lot of those people are from ethnic minority backgrounds and again I think that was very powerful in terms of people's understanding of what makes a community and what makes somebody part of our community, part of our country. That whole thing about putting pictures in the windows was a positive way of uniting people and bringing them together. There's a little girl who lives just down the way here who made a rainbow-coloured pom-pom for every house in her street and it really got neighbours talking to each other.

I absolutely stand with those NHS workers who say it would be good if they were recognised in other ways rather than just applauded and I'm personally irritated by the idea that some people are heroes and some people are not heroes – but actually as a way of bringing people together I thought it worked very well.

Sometimes it's good to sit and share your troubles over a plate of falafel. It reminds me of a poem by another friend from the neighbourhood, the Afghan poet Hasan Bamyani, called 'Darde Dell' – literally, 'Pain Heart':

> Oh, my friend
> let's sit down together and do *darde dell*,
> sharing the pain in our hearts
> I am imprisoned in darkness –
> please shine your light on me
> so I can bloom

I was like a dying flower
during a drought –
you gave me life.
By the help of your hand
I will grow strong again
for the harvest

Instead of bracing myself
against the waves
unleashed by war
I would like to rest
for just a few hours
in the calm waters of a lake

Take my hand
be kind
until I manage to
free myself
from the hostile forces
that bind me

I made my escape
from a volcanic realm
where I suffered like Abraham in Egypt
persecuted by Nimrod
Arriving at the River Nile
I wanted to drink a little water

My generation is waiting for peace
as a swallow waits for spring
but peace has come to me here
With your help I feel
as though I'm living in my motherland
and Oxford becomes

                                        Kabul for me

But in the end, however comforting it is to trade ideas you already share, I am also keen to hear the views of those who voice the unspoken; for whom rainbows remain magical objects. A couple of months after the virus broke, most of us walking through our neighbourhoods hardly glanced at the omnipresent arcs of colour anymore. There are only so many rainbows you can take, I remember telling myself. Yet now, late on the trail, I grow anxious in a street of blank glass – I even find myself hallucinating rainbows, the curved top of a street sign reflected in a window activating my sensor so that my head jerks in its direction. Children lifted up in caves by our ancestors to leave their handprints on the walls were completely present, invested with power by their community; and what I have learnt is that for every hundred or so limp efforts cajoled from the young by parents or teachers there will be one that vibrates with energy, a ritual object made by a member of a tribe still uncontacted by boredom and routine.

The detail that animates an image for me might catch my attention immediately or emerge later. The brick on a porch roof securing the cord from which a rainbow pom-pom hangs. The Buddha sitting patiently in a flowerpot, beneath a bonsaied rosebush. A forlorn garden sculpture, stranded in a desert of gravel. The everyday detritus of looping wires, cracked concrete and rubbish which washes up to our front doors. A rainbow motif painted on newspaper that is twisted in a curve. When I look more closely at this image, I notice the headlines bleeding through the colours: 'Children fight for breath as Amazon fires rage on', one reads, reminding me of that other global pandemic more likely to be fatal to the human race than this. Then an impressionistic, scribbled rainbow framed in the glass of a blue door behind a garden of yellow hollyhocks, emblazoned with the single compound word 'Larkrise'. It seems to encapsulate all the promise of early mornings during this poignantly beautiful summer: of skylarks on hills above the city, miraculously achieving vertical take-off, climbing their unbroken ladder of notes, undiminished by the usual roar of the ring road; of the solo violin part at the beginning of 'Lark Ascending', with its evocation of their song. Rather than demystifying the image, the fact that Larkrise is also the name of a local primary school gives it added pathos. This image is made by an artist who is wishing their isolation over, evoking in one word a vanished world of shouted greetings, teeming corridors and the heady proximity of friends.

Another work replaces the fragility of paper with the solidity of wood: five boards have been nailed together – or, more likely, a construction made for another reason has been repurposed – and a rainbow roughly executed on their stained surface. The outer rings of the bow's arc seem to have been washed out, leaving behind only a trace or tidemark of their presence, while its centre pulses with cerise and magenta. The letters 'NHS' have been scrawled in red in three places and the object placed, leaning against a washing line, on the garden wall. It reminds me of some of the works by African American artists, originally exhibited on porches, in front yards or by the highway for passers-by to see, shown in the exhibition *We Will Walk: Art and Resistance in the American South*.

The charge held by the art in windows is sometimes only revealed when it is converted into a photographic image and studied later. This is when you may see what Roland Barthes in *Camera Lucida* called the 'punctum' of the photograph, which appears independent of the image's ostensible subject; the detail, as Barthes put it, that 'rises from the scene, shoots out of it like an arrow, and pierces me'. Such a detail, he explains, is an addition by the viewer, yet it 'is nonetheless already there'. One such example was situated in a window right next to the pavement on a busy road, fixed to the glass in front of a net curtain. This rainbow has nine different bands of colour moving from black to a washed-out ochre, and the sky in which it floats is stamped with two dark red handprints, their colour not unlike those found in the caves at Chauvet in France. Forced to stand close to the window by the traffic at my heels, and with the afternoon sun falling into the street, I find it impossible to avoid capturing my own reflection and that of objects behind me, the seeker and the sought merging into one. My hands holding the phone are a ghost image behind the handprint on the left, rendered spectral and painterly by the net curtain. The spinning hubcap of a passing car fits exactly into the palm of the handprint on the right, reminding me of petroglyphs from the Three Rivers site in New Mexico that show spirals in the palms of hands, thought to depict healing energy channelled in shamanistic ritual practice.

I decide to retrace my steps to the green-card street and find out what the artists who created the old lady's rainbows can tell me about their meaning. Two of the three sisters in question open the door, the younger of them clearly excited to have a visitor and keen to talk, while her older sibling hangs back, a little more reserved.

Yes, we did those rainbows over the road,

the younger girl says.

I did the one at the side. Our very little sister did the one at the other side and she's only three. Do you want me to tell you who did the rainbows in our window?

And it's true, they have two rainbows in their own window, made out of strips of ruched material.

I did the one at the bottom but it's really faded now, she continues.

Her older sister snorts with derision, finally persuaded to join the conversation.

Actually, I had to do half of it, because you couldn't be bothered,

she says dismissively.

– I did most of it though,

the younger one replies, apparently accustomed to and unfazed by such commentary.

So what does the rainbow mean, do you think, I ask them. The older girl pauses.

Art,

she says.

I write her answer in my notebook. A very good answer, I say. Her younger sister disagrees.

It kind of means stay happy? Because rainbow stuff is to make you feel happy?

But perhaps the most surprising recalibration of the symbol I experience among the half-dozen people I speak to on this particular street is yet to come, when I interview a young mother and her son.

Do you know about the whole significance of rainbows for baby loss?

she asks me.

People who experience a miscarriage often describe the first baby they have after a miscarriage as a rainbow baby – it's what you get after the storm.

– What's a miscarriage?

her young son asks.

I'm ready with a platitude, but the boy's mother obviously believes in parental honesty.

A miscarriage is what happens when you have a pregnancy that doesn't manage to grow properly into an actual baby, she tells him.

– So, like what?

So, the baby that's growing dies inside the mum and it has to come out and not turn into a baby and a person. So, when someone has a miscarriage and then has a happy pregnancy and everything's fine they quite often describe it as their rainbow baby. Quite often you see children dressed in rainbow clothes.

I worry, I have to admit, about the burden placed on these children, wrapped in the unrealised life of another. Do you think their parents are oversharing, I ask her.

Perhaps,

she says.

But I've been through it and it's a very isolating experience.

What do you think the rainbows in people's windows mean, I ask the boy. He looks thoughtful.

I don't know. There's so many ideas. Some people think it helps the doctors and other people think it's not that . . .

This is a street of 'desirable' properties in a good neighbourhood, clearly with a developed sense of community. Riding around the city, it is often streets like this that have the most art still in their windows. What is the relationship ratio between wealth, class and rainbows, I wonder. A friend who works as a social care worker with vulnerable families disabuses me of the idea that the multicoloured symbols were predominantly a middle-class obsession.

At the beginning of lockdown we were completely banned from making home visits unless we were majorly concerned about a child's safety or felt we urgently needed to see the inside of a house or flat,

she tells me.

To make sure we could talk to children on their own we had to make walking visits, outside the home, walking around or sitting on a bench in a park with them. One little girl had a lot to say, a lot of issues, and we used to walk miles together. One of the things I used to do when she got distressed was encourage her to count rainbows. So we walked all around the estates in her area, and I can tell you we saw a *lot* of rainbows.

In the large housing developments straddling the ring road I notice a shift away from solely concentrating on the NHS to supporting essential workers in general, including staff on public transport, those working in supermarkets and delivery drivers.

The window glass in one bungalow's door features a particularly vivid rainbow, obviously created by a child. The woman who emerges seems touched that I am admiring it, as I often find on my travels. The rainbow symbols, with their direct connection to the young, seem to emit a positive energy that deflects suspicion, fear and aggression. The fact that older people often answer the door where one of these symbols is placed suggests that children, through their artwork, are protecting the elderly relatives they are unable to see, until it is safe to visit them once more. The practice of placing protective symbols at windows and the entrances to dwellings goes back a long way and is still prevalent in cultures around the world: the sedum that is planted above gateways to the courtyards of houses in rural Transylvania to prevent the entry of witches, or the dreamcatchers that originated among the Ojibwe and the Lakota peoples and have now become one of the most ubiquitous items of New Age merchandise, placed in children's bedroom windows, are just two examples. This rainbow is stamped with two messages: a 'THANK YOU' in red capitals and a more mysterious message at its lower right-hand extremity, where the bands of colour fragment, that appears to say 'MILK MORE'. The woman and I admire the sign together. It was done, she tells me, by her great-niece.

She was about five when she done it, she's six now,
she tells me.

Why the plea for more milk, I ask.

Because I have a milkman and their name is Milk & More,
she says, pointing down to an empty metal milk crate by
the door.

There were other people on there she thanked – refuse
people and policemen – but a lot of it has faded now.
They're all doing a job and so she put them all on there
for me. I don't want to take them down. I was going to go
over the 'Thank You' but I thought, no, just leave it like
she's done it, she's very good, bless her. She's done another
one over here – that one's for the NHS. 'Thank', it's called,
because she forgot the 'You'! With the little hearts . . . I'll
leave it like that.

In a window on the other side of the road another sign
expressing gratitude to key workers is accompanied by one
marking VE Day, the seventy-fifth anniversary of the end of
the war in Europe, alongside a Union Jack. In view of the
anniversary, the government moved the traditional May bank
holiday from Monday to Friday, perhaps in the hope that, as
well as stimulating consumption, reflection on the outcome
of a previous victory would steel the public's resolve. How
did it all go down behind this door, I wonder.

When a sprightly woman in her seventies answers the
door I begin by asking her why she felt the need to put up a
sign thanking key workers.

One of my granddaughters is one of them for a start,
she tells me.

She's doing assistant nursing at the JR [hospital]. She said
to start with it was very poor, the stuff that they gave them,
but it picked up after a bit and it's OK now. They test them
regular as well. It was quite a dangerous situation to be

in, wasn't it? But then so is driving the bus, quite a lot of bus drivers have come down with it, haven't they? A lot of people in the shops still don't have protection – they don't have those shields on or any glass between them and the customers. And you still get a lot of customers who go in and don't bother with a mask. I tell them off when I see them. Because I think we all should.

You know, you get on the bus and somebody gets on without a mask and I say to them, where's your mask? I say, it's very selfish of you. We're protecting you and you're not bothering to protect us. They usually look a bit embarrassed. But you see if everyone else on the bus who was wearing a mask all turned around and joined in, next time maybe they'd put a mask on! We're too apathetic in this country. If you go to Europe, it's stricter over there. You'd probably get slayed if you didn't wear a mask.

I suspect she would stand behind such summary justice. I ask if the VE Day sign was her contribution to the celebrations. She nods, crossing her arms, surveying the street from her lookout like a British figurehead.

Yes, VE Day, seventy-five years. I stuck 'em up, you know, I thought I'd join in. Sometimes I get a little bit tired of the fact that the people who live here, who've grown up here, whose parents have fought in wars and campaigned for votes for women and jobs and that sort of thing, get left behind – and it's all about the people that have come over here now.

It seems like everything in the news is all about them, there's nothing about us anymore.

And I heard the other day that the Proms, which is on the television, there's been complaints against playing 'Rule Britannia' – and they said they'll play it, but they won't sing the words. And I thought, well come on, you know, I mean, I grew up in the war, surely I can sing 'Rule Britannia', because that's the way I feel? Who can be upset by that? This is our country, if they come here surely they want our country to do well because they're part of it? The words are to do with this country not wanting to be taken over by another country. Now if they come over to this country to live, then surely they feel exactly the same, why would they not? I mean, do they want somebody like China or Iraq or Iran to come over here and turn us into slaves? Is that what they want? We give in too much to these people. They dictate to us and it really is our country. And I get cross about it.

I can see, I tell her, that the words 'Britons never, never, never shall be slaves' would have meant one thing growing up during the war; but surely she'd agree they might mean something different to people now? She laughs good-naturedly but remains unmoved. Having a problem with the words of 'Rule Britannia' is not a matter of age, in her opinion, but of something else entirely. I ask if her Union Jack sign was also put up to mark VE Day.

That's right, that's part of the VE Day and if anyone wants to come and have a chat to me about it, they're perfectly welcome to and I'll tell 'em exactly what I think! If you don't like it here, go somewhere else. We've got people of different nationality connected to our family and I've got friends as well and they don't have all these weird ideas, they just come here to work and be happy and enjoy life. These other people upset it for them, making silly remarks and kicking up over nothing, because when they go out they're looked at in a different way. Come over here by all means, work and make a good living, but accept the country, because that's where you've come to live and be. Don't keep criticising us all the time!

She's still laughing, arms folded, when I press the stop button on my phone and tell her I think I have her views clearly recorded. Why had something in her resolute posture as she stood at her door reminded me of a figurehead? Perhaps because she radiates certainty and connection to a national identity that for her is no less real for being rooted in the past. She is not, of course, alone in her views. Within days, in the face of a hastily stoked culture war in the press and interventions by politicians playing to the gallery of older voters they depend on, the newly appointed Director-General of the BBC has reversed the decision and the words will be sung after all. Perhaps the emanations from this front door have reached Whitehall after all.

III

A DOORSTEP TUTORIAL

They hadn't reached a house I visited a few days later, in a very different neighbourhood near the centre of town. A sign in hand-painted black capitals dominates the front window:

1945

FASCISM

DEFEATED

2020

?

The side window displays a printed poster for the Global Black Caucus: #BLACKLIVES MATTER DEMOCRATS ABROAD and a clenched fist. I knock on the door and the woman who emerges warns me that she is busy, she is writing and hasn't got long.

The banner is a response to VE Day,
she tells me.
I thought I would put up something that reminded people that first of all it wasn't solely a British victory and secondly that it was a victory over fascism which people conveniently forget, especially in these rather parlous

modern times – that's why it has that question mark. I'm a historian who works on this period.

Researching another project, I had been struck with the parallels between the politics of the 1930s and the rise of populism over the past decade or so, but I am wary of making glib comparisons, especially in the company of a historian. Are we seeing a return of fascism to the mainstream in our era, I ask her. The question unlocks a train of thought that is going to keep her from her work for some time.

Historians have been busting their brains on this since Trump was elected,

she says.

We've all been asked to contribute our two penn'orth on whether Trump is a fascist . . . There's a lot of things going on in the politics of America in particular, but to some extent here as well, which are painful reminders that democracy, which we take for granted, can under certain circumstances be very fragile . . . It's not so much that you learn from history but that you think with it, which is a bit different: it's a more critical process; you use the past to think about the present as a sort of intellectual tool.

What people began to remind themselves about in America is that movements like fascism clothe the unfamiliar in the familiar – so they use whatever the local sources of resentment or identification are. Let's take paramilitaries. The paramilitary movements of the interwar Fascists emerged directly from a post-war militarisation of politics whereas the paramilitary impulse in America in the far-right movement comes from a deeply embedded sense that individual freedom is under threat from the state and that the right to bear arms under the Second Amendment is also fragile; that's a very different impulse and produces a different politics. People forget that the Nazis made themselves

37

electable by telling people things they already knew and giving them a Nazi spin, and of course that's what Trump is doing. We know he takes themes that are meaningful to people, like job loss, and ignoble things like the loss of white supremacy, and turns them into campaigns of restoration which are totally illusory.

She turns back to the poster in the window.

So that particular piece of art is a protest against the narrowed version of the celebration of 1945 represented by the celebration of VE Day. I think instead we should be celebrating the election of the Labour government that year as a more important date.

Now she has something to show me and returns inside for a moment, returning with a placard she had made for the American president's visit to Britain. 'No to Trump', the letter 'p' of the president's name spilling over with blood, then the slogan 'Dual Citizen, Dual Shame'. I photograph her holding it, her face obscured by the placard's surface so that her body and the message are one. When she has put it back in the hallway and returns, I mention the conversation I'd had a few days before with someone whose interpretation of VE Day was somewhat different; of her concern that the singing of 'Rule Britannia' might be banned from the Proms, that as a war child she felt ownership of the words 'Britons never, never, never will be slaves'. Once again the subject is irresistible, however strong the call of the work on her desk:

In some senses she is right. The etymology of what the word 'slave' meant in the eighteenth century had an element of subjection to it rather than actually meaning an enslaved person – at that time those words did mean we will not be subject to other peoples, but now the word is tied to the slave trade. You can't control the way that language changes. That song was composed at the height of the slave trade, so it seems to contain a disingenuous aporia at the heart of it – we will never be slaves, but we will certainly make lots of other people slaves!

Two women of a similar age in the same city, each deploying symbols in their windows with vastly different intent. As the historian had explained, 'Slogans are complicated and sometimes one's attitude to them depends on which side you're on; you can endorse a slogan coming from one side that you would repudiate coming from the other, dependent on context.' That's the deal with this town, which comes with a car factory and two universities attached: on one doorstep you receive a lesson in patriotism; on the other a free seminar in historical analysis that includes, as a free bonus, the word 'aporia'. Contained for months within the bubble of my household and the virtual bubble of those I encounter on social media, sifted and selected by who knows what algorithms, I am reminded that Montaigne warned of the dangers of just such a situation, while at the same time proposing a solution:

> Mixing with the world has a marvellously clarifying effect on a man's judgement. We are all confined and pent up within ourselves, and our sight has contracted to the length of our own noses.

I have travelled back in time and am once again outside the house of the VE Day enthusiast. She waves me goodbye as I climb back on my bike and cycle on, searching for markers to respond to. Give me a sign, any sign, I beg the genius loci. What I'm feeling, I suspect, is the melancholy of the anthropologist who has arrived too late. What did I miss at the height of lockdown when people's need to express themselves was greatest and I wasn't paying attention? I console myself with a fragment of Claude Lévi-Strauss, from *Tristes Tropiques*:

> A few hundred years hence, in this same place, another trav-
> eller, as despairing as myself, will mourn the disappearance
> of what I might have seen, but failed to see.

I'm almost ready to head home when I notice a small turning – almost an alley – leading off down to a footpath and
feel an urge to follow it. How does that work, the twitch
in consciousness that, when we bother to listen, serves to
direct our steps? The very last house at the edge of the estate
has three striking images in the window, each bearing a
slogan printed in a different language: 'Andrà tutto bene',
'Vai ficar tudo bem' and 'Everything will be okay', decorated
and fringed with streamers in the colours of their respective
flags. A pregnant woman with a grinning toddler of about
eighteen months at her hip opens the window and asks
me in a strong Portuguese accent what I want. I tell her
I was admiring the artwork in her window and ask her who
made it.

My daughter, she's six years old, she done it,
she says.
Wait a minute, I will get her.
Her daughter appears at the door, a little shy. Do you
speak all three languages, I ask. But she is struck dumb by
my unexpected appearance, so her mother answers for her.
No, only two – Brazilian Portuguese and English. Just little
words in Italian. We have some friends and family in Italy.
– Andrà tutto bene,
the girl says softly, almost to herself, scuffing at something
with her shoe.
That's right,
her mother says.
When I asked her to do this she said she would like to do
it in Italian, Portuguese, English.

That's a really good idea, I say, addressing the girl, who has now stepped out of the house and is poking at some gravel with a stick. What's your name?

My name is Maria Luisa,
she answers with precision.

Did any of your friends make rainbows?
I don't know,
Maria Luisa says.

– She made one rainbow, but he took it off,
her mother says, pointing at the toddler who is now standing in the doorway and who carries on grinning at me.

– It broke, the girl says sadly.

– My sister-in-law, she lives here, her mother says,
but her sister in Italy, she had coronavirus. And every day we pray for Brazil, England and Italy.

I'm struck by the way, after a flight via Brazil, the Italian slogan has landed here, shed its rainbow and taken on its own national colours, alongside the slogans and colours of other nations. Instead of symbols of separation, the respective flags, each resolved into decorative strips of colour, are markers of the daily prayer taking place in this household and clearly intended to speak of shared experience and solidarity. I tell Maria Luisa that her signs are some of the best I have seen in the city and am rewarded by a huge smile.

Not every rainbow artist is of school age. I'm on a different mission, coming to see an elderly friend, in her nineties, who is a resident in a care home. It has been several months since she's been allowed out of the building and when I ask her on the phone how she's been, she replies, 'Oh, fed up.' The words, coming from such a stoic, make me a little anxious. I have been allowed to book a slot and meet her in a separate room, just the two of us, as long as I wear a visor and keep a distance. I am met at the main entrance, and after I have washed my hands and my temperature has been taken I am issued with a visor and led around the outside of the building to the room where she is waiting, which has its own outside door that we are told we must keep open, despite the chill.

Our chairs have been positioned several feet apart. It is six months since we have seen each other face to face and it is a little awkward, me in my ridiculous headwear, our not being able to approach each other or embrace, but once she has returned to her room to retrieve the hearing aids she has forgotten and rejoined me, the conversation flows. Certain people serve to connect us to the past in a visceral way, not really because of how they are or what they say, but simply through their presence in a room. She has a special place in my affection because she was my mother's best friend from childhood and remained her best friend throughout her life, even though they lived separated by distance for years. We both feel the loss of her. And so we sit together, each catching a glimpse of the same absence in the other.

As I am escorted out once more and divested of my visor, I notice a rainbow stuck to the glass in the window of the entrance that I hadn't noticed when I arrived. Was it another example of a talisman against the virus made by a child, I wondered, sent to protect an elderly relative? It turns out the woman who is escorting me runs activities for the residents as part of her role; she had asked them to make rainbows and write poems to accompany them. This was done by a 92-year-old woman, she tells me, but the poem isn't her own. In fact the words are William Wordsworth's, familiar but given added poignancy here.

> My heart leaps up when I behold
> A rainbow in the sky:
> So was it when my life began;

> So is it now I am a man;
> So be it when I shall grow old,
> Or let me die!

I cycle back through the city in chill sunshine. I am, I realise, speaking under my breath to people no longer on the planet, and I feel their presence around me even as I move through space, thanking them and acknowledging my debts.

On the other side of the river, as I dodge the rain, my eye is caught by a remarkable design in a window: a rocket somewhat reminiscent in shape to the one featured in Georges Méliès's 1902 film *Le Voyage dans la Lune* – except this one is decorated with a vivid rainbow stripe and features a riveted porthole as well as a sickle moon and a star, both coloured in gold. The artist in question has created a rainbow emblem that blasts off to arrive in the post-moonshot age, while remaining charmingly retro in its design. In the window above, a card bears the words 'Thank You' and a blue street sign on the wall in Arabic and English reads 'Tahrir Square'. I ring the bell and hear a young voice call, 'I'll get it.' The girl who opens the door, her mother behind her, glances at her work.

It was basically the rainbow idea, but I didn't want to just do a normal rainbow,

she says.

So what does it mean, this rocket?

I wasn't quite sure at the time, but I guess it was just, going up?

So, hope perhaps?

Yeah.

And the 'Thank You' in the window . . .?

She loses her composure for a moment and raises a hand to stifle a giggle.

I actually got that as a card sent to me by someone else, but we put it there to thank everyone who's helped out.

A bit of gratitude recycling, I suggest. They both nod, then her mother says:

We've been thanking the NHS and key workers.

We've been thanking bin men for example and people who work in shops – bus drivers, we've been giving the thumbs up to bus drivers.

After discussion, we agree that the proper name for her creation is the Rainbow Rocket of Hope. Finally, I have to ask about the street sign for Tahrir Square, the site of the huge demonstrations that looked as though they would change Egypt's course forever, now come to rest in a quiet British street.

Her father's half Egyptian and she spent the first few years of her life in Cairo,

her mother says,

and we lived through and participated in the uprising. Well, she didn't –

daughter and mother turn to each other –

no, actually you did, we took you to Tahrir Square, yeah.

The girl laughs with her mother and I tell her what an amazing thing it is to be able to say that she'd been present at those events. She nods, but she is serious again, still thinking about the rocket.

I think it's basically showing everyone that you're part of the whole thing and you're trying to show that everyone's going through it,

she says.

Another interpretation, sincerely given. I'm beginning to feel as though I am in a vast field experiment in semiotics, a labyrinth of symbols. But what if no one can agree on what those symbols mean?

44

IV

THE CAPTURED BANNER

And what if a community feels a symbol has been stolen from them?

Artist, writer and curator Alex Noble is clear about what has happened over the course of the pandemic. We meet at his home in Margate, a house which is devoid of slogans on the outside, apart from a very small, typed message on the door knocker which reads:

d
r
a
w
i
n
g
s

a
r
e

t
h
o
u
g
h
t
s

He laughs when I mention it, explains he likes to leave his poems in the environment. We start talking about the symbols that have appeared in windows over the past few months but time is short, so I book a slot to continue our conversation when I'm back at my desk.

I'd noticed rainbow flags going up early on,
he tells me down the line a few days later,
 and I'd said to people who I'd organised Pride with, we're going into lockdown and the whole world's gone gay and it's quite sweet! There was something calming about the fact that suddenly our symbology had appeared everywhere – with something bad happening, our presence had increased. But then it was a few more weeks into lockdown and the experience for everyone had got much heavier and there was no end in sight and it was obvious we were in pretty murky waters – we'd gone into lockdown with the idea that this might go on for a number of weeks and then a number of weeks went by and it was suddenly evident that we didn't know how long it was going to be, more people were dying and it was at that point that I must have looked around and seen the rainbows everywhere and taken in my environment and it just suddenly felt ominous. It was an unnerving, unsettling feeling and it was very much something a gay person, or someone who is other, would recognise from being in environments where you're the only one and potentially that's not OK, because you're not accepted. It was that sudden realisation that the symbol didn't belong to my community anymore and the importance of that symbol was amplified because it had been taken away so quickly and with such little thought for the community it was predominantly used by. And knowing that it would never be given any thought or discussion by greater society. So that was the first time I really vocalised

it. Something had been taken away and I was made to feel
unsafe by that action.

Alex's words make sense when you consider that the rainbow flag has been associated with the LGBTQIA+ community
for more than four decades. In 1978 Harvey Milk, San Francisco
City Supervisor and the first openly gay person to be elected
as a public official in California, asked his friend Gilbert Baker
to design a unifying symbol for the gay community. As well
as being an artist, Baker was a cabaret performer and a dab
hand with a sewing machine – he was, as he put it, 'the drag
queen that couldn't afford the clothes I liked so I had to make
them all'. His response was partly shaped by the events of the
preceding two years: the impact of the Watergate scandal, the
ignominious withdrawal from Vietnam and the celebration
of the Republic's bicentenary in 1976. The public response
to these conflicting impulses had been to festoon the nation
with the Stars and Stripes. Baker didn't necessarily feel represented by that national symbol, but, as he told a curator in
2015, something stirred in his imagination . . .

And I thought, a flag is different than any other form of
art. It's not a painting, it's not just cloth, it is not just a
logo – it functions in so many different ways. I thought
that we needed that kind of symbol, that we needed as a
people something that everyone instantly understands. [The
Rainbow Flag] doesn't say the word 'Gay', and it doesn't
say 'the United States' on the American flag but everyone
knows visually what they mean. And that influence really
came to me when I decided that we should have a flag, that
a flag fitted us as a symbol, that we are a people, a tribe
if you will. And flags are about proclaiming power, so it's
very appropriate.

The only symbol that had been used for gay identity before this time had been the pink triangle gays were forced to wear in Nazi Germany. The gay community had defiantly adopted them in the post-war period, repurposing the emblem from an indicator of shame, as it was intended to be, to one of pride. Nevertheless, Baker felt it was no longer appropriate.

> It came from such a horrible place of murder and holocaust and Hitler. We needed something beautiful, something from us. The rainbow is so perfect because it really fits our diversity in terms of race, gender, ages, all of those things. Plus, it's a natural flag – it's from the sky!

On another occasion, Baker's words were darker, hinting at the struggle and suffering from which this symbol was born and why those who own it are not happy to have it taken from them. A true flag is not something you can really design, he is said to have remarked. A true flag is torn from the soul of the people.

When Alex started reaching out to friends in the community, he found he wasn't the only one left with a sense of foreboding by the way the rainbow had been recoded. Like many others, he was upset that annual Pride events had been cancelled because of social distancing requirements, compounding the feeling of erasure. As Baker put it:

> Our job as gay people (is) to come out, to be visible, to live in the truth as I say, to get out of the lie. A flag really fits that mission, because that's a way of proclaiming your visibility, or saying, 'This is who I am!'

Even more alarming to observers was the speed with which corporate sponsors of Pride events rebranded the merchandise they had created for Pride – including rainbow flags – as being in support of the NHS. In a matter of days, six-striped Pride flags appeared on eBay as 'Thank You NHS Flag Large 5 x 3 FT – Front Line Workers Banner Charity GBP 5.69'. A man on Twitter shared that his grandfather, not usually a man of progressive views, had planted one outside his house.

As an artist and curator, Alex responded to such appropriations, however well meaning, in the only way he could.

I had a commission to do an exhibition during Pride and the penny dropped that I could use that space for a collaborative piece, so that artists, not just me, could comment on it and make a creative response. So I put the information out and it really resonated with the artists and that was important, that we shared feelings about it.

The exhibition *Red Flags* took the form of a contributive installation in the window of The Margate School, an independent art school housed in the old Woolworths building in Margate. It featured red flags made by invited artists, each bringing their own message of resistance and solidarity, that combined into one visual statement, raised against the disempowering forces unleashed against the community during lockdown. It was accompanied by a sound piece by Noble in which the voices of contributing artists made both poetic and literal responses to the work and its context.

On the poster for the exhibition, the word 'RED' going vertically down the page is the backbone of an acrostic: Representation, Education, Disruption. 'Everywhere we look there is a signal, a warning, a minefield exploding around us,' the press release reads, 'the very fabric of society is being dismantled and reformed as we see the reappropriation of cultural symbols and the dismantling of historical statues.'

The words somehow encapsulate another pervasive feeling – that we have reached the end of the road. The virus has

49

forensically exposed the incompetence and corruption that exist at the top of society along with the existential threats facing the planet; surely, many feel, we can move on from this – reset our values and priorities in the way we did at the end of the Second World War, for instance, when the National Health Service was born? Yet instead it feels as though we remain suspended, with the normal rules on hold. No one knows how long we will have to live with the effects of the virus; this suits the narcissistic, clown-like men who rule country after country around the world, stuffing the pockets of their cronies with contracts rushed through without scrutiny under emergency rulings to provide services they are eminently unqualified to deliver. Gramsci had it about right in his prison notebooks: 'The crisis consists precisely in the fact that the old is dying and the new cannot be born; in this interregnum a great variety of morbid symptoms appear.' Don't they just.

So first of all the rainbow symbol is appropriated from Pride, I say to Alex, when it is used as a symbol in support of the NHS. Then it is taken back from the public by corporations rebranding themselves with messages in support of the NHS, the trains with their new rainbow liveries and all the rest . . .

Then the same thing happens again,

Alex says,

when the government takes it on and all their messaging suddenly becomes centred around what had been a civil act or protest; and then the government are wearing rainbow badges, that's where the propaganda bit comes in . . . And we're all essentially clapping for the government's bad management. We can't seem to acknowledge the fact that they have let down one of our most important systems and that everything's failing – we're clapping to express support for that! Solidarity with failure.

Solidarity with failure: it sounds very British, somehow; or, at least, redolent of a Britain those who govern us threaten we will return to if they are forced from power. Yet, in the unforgiving light of the pandemic, it is they who appear to have failed, at the hour of our greatest need.

But I am still pondering the slipperiness of a symbol that has morphed from a representation of the pride and identity of a marginalised community into a more general emblem of hope during a global crisis, finally ending up in Britain specifically as an expression of solidarity with health workers. In its ability to spread across continents, attach itself to different causes and shift our perception of what it represents, this particular rainbow has behaved more like a virus than a flag.

Its mutation in the UK may have been triggered by a report published in November 2018 by the campaigning organisation Stonewall. A survey of five thousand respondents revealed that depression and anxiety were shockingly high among the LGBTQIA+ community – a staggering one in ten Trans people had attempted suicide over the previous twelve months – and one in four who had sought treatment in the NHS had experienced negative remarks from healthcare staff about their sexuality. Evelina Children's Hospital in London responded by producing, and encouraging staff to wear, rainbow NHS badges to show that their hospital was an open, safe, inclusive and non-judgemental place. The health secretary tweeted a picture of the badges accompanied by the words: 'Love this. Wear mine with pride.' (He has continued to do so, delivering each new contradictory briefing with it in his lapel.) The initiative begun at the Evelina spread throughout much of the NHS in 2019, the badges a common sight on staff uniforms, so that when the virus took hold, the link between the rainbow and the NHS was already established in the public mind.

Sometimes this slippage between meanings has unexpected consequences. I'm back at the table outside the falafel bar, in conversation with my friend, who works at a university. Discussing the way in which the Pride banner has been appropriated reminds him of the experience of one of his students.

Because of lockdown he had to go home and when he got home he saw that there was a rainbow flag hanging from the house and he thought, blimey, my little brother must have come out!

He knew his brother was gay and he was really pleased that while he'd been away he'd found the courage to come out. He finally said something – I can't remember exactly what it was, but he suggested that the rainbow flag was referring to his brother's sexuality – and then he had to spend the next week trying to undo what he'd said. Eventually, because of this misunderstanding – or misreading of the symbolism – his brother did come out and in the end it was all OK, but it was a really big deal for everyone involved and it wouldn't have happened if he hadn't come home from university and seen the rainbow flag.

V

STICKY BLOOD

I've been meaning for a while to have a proper conversation with a friend who worked as an intensive care nurse on a Covid ward throughout the first lockdown; she is one of those we have sanctified through our window worship and with offerings of applause on our doorsteps. I want to get a sense of what really happened on what people call the front line; and what it felt like to be the object of so much veneration when the service she worked for was in crisis.

It's a question of catching her between shifts and the rounds of study she is doing for a new qualification that she hopes will eventually lead to a change of career. When we finally sit down together I'm struck by the anger she still feels at how events have been handled and the lives that have been lost as a result. At the same time she has the air of someone who has been on an arduous and at times terrible journey but has come back with memories she wouldn't trade with anyone. When she begins to speak the words come fast, in an almost unbroken stream.

I got sick of white men in suits telling us how we were going to do this, because white men in suits is not what you see in the NHS: we are Black, we are Asian, we are everything – we are *not* white men in suits.

The constant rhetoric about the number of ventilators they were going to buy drove us all nuts. It doesn't matter how many ventilators you've got if you don't have nurses to look after those patients, and doctors to work with those patients, and physiotherapists to work with those patients. You don't put someone on a ventilator and shove them in a room: somebody has to manipulate the settings on that ventilator to make sure it's appropriate for that patient, somebody has to sort out their food, clean their teeth, empty their catheter bag, give them the drugs they need in order to maintain their blood pressure . . . All of those things are very skilled, yet nobody mentioned intensive care nurses, it was all about ventilators and hospital beds, and I was wondering where is the team going to come from to manage it all?

When I go into work I know exactly the skill set of the people around the room. I am often put in charge of the bay that I'm in, so I know that if that particular nurse gets a dialysis machine she's very new to it and she'll need a lot of support; if that patient isn't very well that nurse will need a level of support but the nurse in the corner will be fine because he's amazing. That whole dynamic just got lost and that's very devaluing to what we do. That you think you can just buy enough ventilators and the problem will be solved – they wasted so much money on that. So much money, and it was soul-destroying watching that whole discussion.

At the same time there was a huge amount of publicly expressed love and support. How did it feel to be on the receiving end of that? Were you comfortable with all the rainbows and clapping, for instance?

The local community were amazing,
she says.

One shift a load of cakes arrived, and it was the parents of kids at a school who had all clubbed together and bought cakes for us. And you just think, wow, thanks for thinking of us. We often got sent food and other things and we really appreciated all of it.

But I found the clapping very difficult – the 'Oh, well done for going to work'. What did you think I was going to do? If work texts me and says we have a major incident, I will be on my bike and up the road in five minutes. We don't ever leave each other to deal with these situations; it is about the patients, but it's also about my colleagues – we deal with it, we pull together and sort it out. And all that goodwill is what's being stripped out of the NHS because we feel so undervalued.

I didn't need people standing on their doorsteps clapping; I just wanted people to appreciate how difficult it was and to hold the government to account.

Going into that kind of environment you have to take your whole self to work. You can't do it unless you're prepared to be fully in the moment, in the situation, with the family and the patient. I deal with families in the most stressful situation that you will ever find yourself in, when your loved one is seriously unwell and needs surgery or has had a cardiac arrest; we have a lot of people who die on our unit and you cannot deal with that without being fully present with those families and going through it with them. They're not just bodies, they are people with hopes and dreams and expectations of how long they would live or how long they would have with a loved one . . .

Normally in intensive care we work one nurse to one patient, and we have thirty nurses on a shift and that's fine. But during Covid they said, we're sorry we don't have enough nurses, so we were working with two or three patients at a time and Covid patients are really sick. We tried to sort it out, we got a lot of nurses from A & E and trauma, which went really quiet because people were staying at home, and from the children's ward, but they weren't ICU nurses so they weren't trained in everything we have to do, so the pressure then fell on you: you'd be working with three really sick patients with a nurse who didn't really know what she was doing, it was really hard and it was a completely different environment. Usually we look after people really nicely in ICU, we clean their teeth every shift and we make sure their skin stays beautiful and we check all their pressure areas – we do all the technical stuff but we do all the care as well – but we just didn't have time. We usually roll people over at least every four hours to make sure their back's OK, make sure they're not getting a sore, but during Covid sometimes we only did it once during a shift of six or eight hours and it was hard knowing we were compromising our usual standards of care.

Apart from the shortage of staff and the sheer volume of patients you had to deal with, what were the particular challenges you faced?

It's very complicated with Covid, because once you've gone in with your PPE you've got to stay in for two hours, you can't come out – the logistics were a nightmare. We would have to text through: can we have a new tube of this or box of that? Even getting food for patients was really hard, you couldn't use crockery because you couldn't wash it up and nobody wanted to take it afterwards so it took us a couple of weeks to work out how to do all this. We had an airlock where you go in to make sure the air gets pulled into the unit and not out of the unit, so we'd put things in the airlock for each other. We had to be divided, each shift into two teams, team one inside and team two outside the airlock. On one particular night shift I was outside, sorting out something on the computer, I must have been going through the drug regime, working out what drugs we needed. I think I was the team leader for that night. Then we got a phone call and were told that team two needs to go in, a patient's arrested. It takes fifteen minutes usually to put the PPE on but we did it in a couple of minutes and I was running in, saying, which patient is it, and it was a young woman. She'd just been admitted, she was on oxygen and she'd been chatting, she hadn't needed to be intubated. Now there were eight people around the bed trying to do CPR, so I said, what do you need, and they gave me a blood sample to put through the machine to find out what was going on. And I put the sample through and as I did I realised she had the same date of birth as me. Ohhh . . .

she pauses for a moment,

it was one of the worst resusses I've been on, because we all knew how young she was, she had two children, we knew this already because she'd been chatting to one of the others about her family; she'd been fine but she deteriorated rapidly. She had a complication of Covid where she had a profuse infection, but we didn't understand why she had an arrest.

When you've connected with somebody and you've had a laugh with them and you've made them a cup of tea and met their needs you do get that emotional closeness to them, you feel like you're invested in them – when they talk about their family and their hopes and dreams it's very hard when they die.

Why did some younger patients who didn't appear to have other health problems suffer so badly with Covid, I ask.

A lot had problems with blood clots – many younger patients died of pulmonary embolism, clot on the lung, including those who were told to stay at home and subsequently died. Covid makes the blood really sticky. In the first few days of treating it, we suddenly realised that when you put a patient on a dialysis machine, after about half an hour all the pressures on the machine would start going up and then it would clot. Usually you leave someone on dialysis for seventy-six hours, so we were thinking, what's going on? I remember one shift, setting up three or four dialysis machines, they have massive five-litre bags and I was lifting these bags up onto the machines and sweating in my PPE. We had to keep putting patients on dialysis because of blood clots; the doctors would come along and put in a line in the artery to measure the blood pressure and enable us to take regular blood samples and I would have to phone them an hour later and say, I'm sorry, that arterial line has clotted. There's something about the virus that causes coagulation.

The talk of sticky blood reminds me of an elderly relative of my own who was losing her memory gradually and was told that very small bubbles in her blood caused by her irregular heartbeat were erasing parts of her memory as they circulated through her brain. The thought of those tiny destructive bubbles sent out to do their work with every beat of her heart was disturbing. This in turn reminds me of a friend who had Covid and found that for some time after he got better, he struggled to remember simple instructions at work . . . Even as I utter these observations, I realise that, given my complete lack of medical knowledge, I can't be making much sense, but she listens patiently.

Most patients we woke up after they'd been on the ventilator were very confused,
she tells me.
They stay with us about twenty-four hours after we take
the tube out because they still need quite a lot of care.
One of them beckoned me over and obviously thought
I was his wife or something and he said, there's a tenner
in the kitchen, do you want to go out and get a bottle
of wine, love? And I felt like saying to him, yes, that is
the best suggestion anyone has made the whole shift.
I'm going!
The guy who really cheered us all up was called Andy. He
was really young and not fat, I don't know how he ended
up with Covid, a nice chap, we extubated him and took
him off the ventilator and he was really good for the first
couple of hours, but then he kept trying to get out of bed
and every time we'd go over and say you need to stay in
bed, you mustn't get out of bed and he'd say, yeah yeah,
that's fine, but as soon as you'd walk away he'd be getting
out of bed again. I was a bit exasperated because I had so
much to do and I went over and said, Andy, what's up?
Tell me what we can do to make you more comfortable,
so you'll stay in bed. And he looked at me and said, you've
all got little green hats and I haven't got one. So I said,
I can fix that. I went to the trolley and got one of the
green theatre hats we all wear and I said, here you go,
and showed him how to put it on and he was happy, he
didn't get out of bed again. It was almost as if he needed
to belong and wanted to be like everybody else. He didn't
wake up and say, where am I, you're all in strange outfits,
what am I doing here, he was quite happy with where he
was, he just couldn't get over that he didn't have a green
hat like everyone else. And I thought, that's what it's all

about, it's the little things that are important. We make everyone feel like they belong.

There's so much unknown about the effects of the virus. Oxford is doing a study to follow people up – you had to be hospitalised to take part, presumably because at the beginning they were only testing people in hospitals, but they're looking at cognitive function and one of the research nurses told me that one of the tests is to draw a clock face and then draw the hands to the clock. One man drew the clock and then put the hands outside the clock, he couldn't work out where the hands went, yet she'd had a perfectly normal conversation with him minutes before. So it definitely affects cognitive function.

She's been keen to talk, keen to make sure that her memories, at least, are not lost; and what is plain to me as we stand up is that she is proud to have been there during this moment, when her colleagues and her patients needed her.

I wouldn't have had it any other way,

she says.

Even if I'd changed careers by the time this happened, I probably would have gone back.

She thinks for a moment.

Of course I would, because I have the skills. That's what we do.

VI

OF NAMING AND MONUMENTS

I almost missed it. Returning from searching the windows of a particular neighbourhood I notice a monument set back from the road and partly concealed by the overhanging branches of a tree. The stone obelisk marks the end of a previous national calamity, the words chiselled into its surface already almost illegible as weather and lichen continue their work of erasure. A clue to its meaning is given by the words etched on its front:

GREATER LOVE
HATH NO
MAN THAN THIS
THAT A MAN
LAY DOWN
HIS LIFE FOR HIS
FRIENDS

The quotation from the Gospel of John was habitually used for memorials to soldiers who died in the First World War. Situated yards from the entrance to what would normally be a busy primary school, for the most part unnoticed by those who walk and drive past it, the obelisk is a little over a century old. It is harder to make out the names of the fallen, but here are a few:

PTE T.C. DEARLOVE 1ST 4TH O.B.L.I.
PTE. P.I. EVANS 8TH GLOS. REGT.
RIFLEMAN R. FAULKNER 2ND BATT K.R.R.C.
1ST CLASS STOKER C. HARTWELL R.N.R
SERGEANT MAJR SHRIMPTON

Dearlove; Evans; Faulkner; Hartwell; Shrimpton: those names would have had a powerful effect a century ago; not only on those living in the neighbourhood who knew the men personally, but to anyone who saw them, on a psychological level. Over the months following the arrival of the virus we grew accustomed to the daily figures broadcast in the media of new cases and fatalities, all nameless. As long as they remain mere statistics, those who die are easier to dismiss, consigned to the void with the words 'well, they were old, they had lived a full life', or 'they were overweight', 'they had underlying health conditions', 'they would have died sometime anyway'. It is only when the dead are given names and faces, when the virus touches down in our street, our family or house, that our eyes are opened. The friend and neighbour, whose older sister dies aged fifty-one, in a Midlands city: Allah decided her time had come, I am told. Another friend in his thirties, a filmmaker who got the virus before lockdown and didn't know what it was until weeks later when it became known that loss of taste and smell were symptoms; when we meet he tells me he still has days when he struggles to get to the end of a paragraph without his brain shutting down, as he puts it, and he feels overcome with the urge to close his eyes. No one knows if these effects will be permanent.

It is only when the dead are memorialised with photographs and biographies in national newspapers that we begin to grasp, momentarily at least, how many health professionals have died, from doctors and consultants to ancillary staff and hospital porters (greater love hath no man than this); how the virus has exposed the deep health inequalities in society; and perhaps most strikingly, how those from Black and minority ethnic backgrounds are disproportionately affected.

Unlike those who raised the obelisk, we have not been through a war – but one name that circulated around the world during lockdown exposed another war that many would say has been going on in Western countries for hundreds of years: the war the state has waged against Black people. 'Say his name,' the crowds protesting the death of George Floyd chanted in streets around the world, 'Say his name.' Not only did we say his name, not only did his face appear in windows, on walls, posters and signs held aloft, but if we chose to, if we could bear to, we watched his death in the safety of our own homes, over and over again. 'I don't remember seeing an image that harks back so graphically to Mantegna's *Dead Christ*,' said Black British artist John Akomfrah in an online conversation during lockdown in June. 'I don't recall seeing anything which felt so graphically like the scene of a crucifixion, so I'm not entirely surprised by its galvanising force, power and zeal.'

Those of us called on to question our white privilege could reflect that, although leaving our front doors now brought other, invisible dangers, we were statistically far less likely to be searched, harassed, questioned about our reasons for being present in the world at all, let alone strangled in plain sight. The blankness of Derek Chauvin's gaze as he knelt on Floyd's neck and stared down the young woman filming him is the blankness of complicity in a system reflected back at those of us who have failed to effectively challenge it for far too long.

'This great world,' Montaigne wrote, 'is the mirror into which we must look if we are to behold ourselves from the proper standpoint.' God, how we hated what we saw.

'Daddy changed the world,' Floyd's six-year-old daughter said as she was carried through the streets on the shoulders of his friend Stephen Jackson, and one of the ways it seems her words will be borne out is that the presence of malignant spectres from the past, in the form of statues on our buildings and in our streets – images that for centuries have thrown shadows of past infamies onto the present and into the future – will be tolerated no longer. In Bristol the statue of the slave trader Edward Colston was pitched into the harbour; in Oxford the High Street was filled with protesters demanding the statue of imperialist and white supremacist Cecil Rhodes be taken down from its position over the entrance to Oriel College.

It is perhaps difficult for those who oppose such radical change to understand the impact memorials have on the lives of those directly affected by the legacies they commemorate. For artist John Akomfrah, works like the image of Colston 'in a very mystical way contaminate the spaces in which [the statues] were born'. He is not alone in being sensitive to their malevolence. For family worker Darren, an aficionado of film and television drama, the statue of Cecil Rhodes at the heart of his own city recalls an episode of a much-loved TV show.

There was a story on *Doctor Who* that scared me and scared my kids when they were younger,

he tells me.

It was an episode called *The Weeping Angels* – one of those lightning-in-a-bottle things where the writer nailed it and the actors nailed it and it worked. The premise of the story was that when you look at them these beings are absolutely still, they are like statues, but if you blink or if the light goes off, they creep up on you and drain your life. Now if I'm going through a city and see statues I wonder if they're weeping angels hiding in plain sight that can't move. What happens if you blink, what happens if it gets dark, could they turn on you?

I think with that Cecil Rhodes statue, it's a case of 'we see you for who you are now'. You might have been looking over our city in the past but we really see you now and we know that in those dark places you're draining the lives of the citizens, even though many of them don't even know that you're part of the city. I did a catering A level as a kid and had a part-time job for three years in Oriel College kitchens, but I never knew the statue was there – yet it's been so influential. When there are things that become intrinsic to a city's narrative, people say, we acknowledge these people were bad, but we can't afford for them to be bad, we depend on them so much. For every time you say you can't afford to come to terms with the nature of these objects, just remember there's somebody on the other end of that decision who is suffering from the humiliation it causes.

His words remind me of something James Baldwin said in an appearance on *The Dick Cavett Show* in 1968, later included in Raoul Peck's film *I Am Not Your Negro*, about the lasting impact in America of the legacy of slavery. As usual Baldwin spoke fast and precisely, his eyebrows often raised in seeming incredulity at the facts he himself was relating, delivering every now and then a statement of such condensed poetic power as to leave his interlocutor stunned into silence. As when he told Cavett, 'All your buried corpses now begin to speak.'

What Darren has said about the psychological impact of oppressors' statues on the living is borne out in the personal accounts of countless people from places as far apart as Belgium, where images of King Leopold II are being toppled, Mexico, where statues of Columbus and other symbols glorifying the colonial past are meeting the same fate, and the American South, where the presence of Confederate statues, long a familiar part of the environment, is now being contested. It's time, as Darren says, to see the historical figures we choose to commemorate for who they are.

We've agreed to meet at a lock on the river where there are benches and we can talk in the open air. The architecture of the lock reminds me of the Bristol waterfront and we begin by discussing the statue of slave trader Edward Colston that was thrown into the harbour there. It seemed so just to me, I say, because of the people that would have been jettisoned alive from his ships during the Middle Passage, and I'm sorry to say this (I'm aware I'm overexcited and we've only just met) but did you know sharks changed their migration route so they could follow the slave ships?

Really,

he says,

I never heard that before. The more people hear stories like that the better, because it will get them animated. It helps to visualise these things . . .

He thinks for a moment.

But you could turn it round and say humanity lost its moral direction and changed *its* migration route to capitalise on the slave trade. There were sharks feeding at sea, but there were humans feeding on land who were willing to abandon all humanity for the profit they could make. They needed to set up a narrative to enable people to do that. First of all, let's say that the people we enslave are not human; if you can sell that to the public then you can use these people

to pick cotton and base all kinds of textile industries on
that . . . At least sharks are more honest, they're saying, we
want to eat your flesh! A shark is such a metaphor among
human beings for a predator . . .
Metaphors are one thing; emotion is another.
I'm angry,
Darren says,
me, Darren, I'm angry about a story about my parents
and my forefathers of which I don't know all the details.
I know that if I'm a Black person who's come through the
Caribbean there's a high possibility I've come from slave
stock. Yes, I know my parents' story, I kind of know my
grandparents' story, but I don't know the story of their
grandparents, who would have been slaves . . . and beyond
that I don't know anything. So I'm angry about a story
I don't know, even though I know that story's true. How
do I deal with that, how do I articulate it? I think that's
what's starting now, that people are getting the tools to
say, OK, I'm sharing with you that Black lives matter. I'm
not telling you that you have to believe that, but if you
want to share in my life, in my experience, I'm asking for
you to listen. I know you're not listening if you shout at
me: 'Well, all lives matter. White lives matter as well, don't
they?' I'm not saying white lives don't matter, I'm trying
to share with you something that has a four-hundred-year
history, about white privilege –
he pauses for a moment, a trifle wearily –
but when you talk about white privilege, these people say,
'I ain't got no privilege'!
All of this stuff that's been happening,
he continues,
the institutional racism, has been an ongoing bad dream, an
ongoing nightmare, but now we're getting an awakening;

the question, now we're waking up, is how do we practically start changing things?

Covid has that political dynamic to it. George Floyd is connected to Covid, because if you live in communities that are poor, if you don't have access to good healthcare, if you don't have access to good nutrition, these things cause underlying health issues and the health issues make you vulnerable to Covid. Class and inequality and race all intersect. If you're on the bottom rungs of the ladder for race reasons or class reasons or both, it's going to have an impact. So why are there more bus drivers who are Black than white; why are we in more low-paid jobs than white people? One question leads to another question. When you follow through all of these questions you begin to see this really big picture of inequality. These things are institutional, and the way George Floyd was treated is institutional, so people are connecting the dots and that's what's powerful.

These connections are powerfully expressed in a statement called 'The Universal Right to Breathe', issued early in the pandemic by the Cameroonian philosopher Achille Mbembe. He writes:

Before this virus humanity was already threatened with suffocation. If war there must be, it cannot so much be against a specific virus as against everything that condemns the majority of humankind to a premature cessation of breathing, everything that fundamentally attacks the respiratory tract, everything that, in the long reign of capitalism, has constrained entire segments of the world population, entire races, to a difficult, panting breath and life of oppression. To come through this constriction would mean that we conceive of breathing beyond its purely biological aspect,

and instead as that which we hold in-common, that which,
by definition, eludes all calculation. By which I mean, the
universal right to breath.

Darren and I are interrupted momentarily by a boat that
has entered the lock; a small cruiser, of the type that can be
hired for the day, is crammed with young people dancing and
singing along to a soundtrack of upbeat dance tracks, holding
glasses and bottles aloft. We agree that there doesn't seem to
be much social distancing going on aboard, although we do
notice there seem to be only six people responsible for the
impressive volume of noise (we are living at the time under
a regime christened by the government as 'The Rule of Six');
but then we notice a seventh young woman who is operating
the lock. A minor infringement, in the cause of Good Times.
It lifts the spirits to see a group of people so determined to
enjoy themselves, living in the moment beneath a September
sun that feels increasingly like a miraculous last blessing as
the nights draw in. For now, they remain a defiant bubble of
happiness, floating out of earshot on a river that goes all the
way to the sea and back into history, to a time when Britannia
ruled the waves. And this also, as one of the characters says at
the beginning of Conrad's *Heart of Darkness*, has been one of
the dark places of the earth. And, once the pleasure boat has
receded into the distance, if you stay quiet and still, you can
sense that darkness reaching upriver all the way from where
Conrad's characters sat on their ship in the wide estuary to
where we are now.

We return to the way history has been controlled for so
long by people who seem reluctant to hand over the keys to
the library.

How do they lie to us? All the guys who say these things
have learnt to do rhetoric,

Darren says.

All the skills that are used to cause division, most of them are the tools of Empire; there's an expectation that what they have learnt belongs to the ruling class. These tools – of rhetoric, for instance – I see them lacking in my community; that's not a criticism, the ruling class are only 7 to 10 per cent of the population anyway so they aren't only not in my community, there's a lot of communities they're not in.

That's why I'm hopeful about Black Lives Matter, because people are having to learn new ways to speak; this generation who've seen the death of George Floyd are learning very quickly and we'll see them get the message out in new ways. In the next five to ten years they will have got how to organise and protest under their belts. Because if you want to do it with integrity and it's not about just shouting and rioting – not that I'm saying there's anything wrong with rioting, I understand why it happens – there are skills that have to be learnt: how do you gather people together, especially now you're less likely to have a leadership figure? There isn't the Malcolm or the Martin, there isn't that person who gives a clear 'this is what we're going to do'. If you want to bring about real change you need leadership, people who understand that leadership is a role and it doesn't mean 'I'm the boss'. I'm enthused, because I think in the next ten years we'll see those leaders emerge.

It's only later, on the way home, that I recall that there has been controversy over whether the trade changed the migration routes of sharks, not least since the idea was referenced in a speech by Representative Donald M. Payne in Congress on the occasion of the bicentenary of the trade's abolition in 2007. My computer confirms that

Payne correctly identified the movement of enslaved people across the Atlantic as the greatest forced migration in the history of the world, but unfortunately quadrupled the number of people historians now believe were involved, giving slavery deniers an opportunity to dismiss everything else he said. Am I just another gullible liberal, as the trolls would doubtless suggest, taken in by a historical myth? The shark was certainly a powerful symbol for abolitionists, as well as for Romantic authors like the poet James Thomson, who evoked it in language of terrifyingly intensity in his poem 'Summer':

> Here dwells the direful shark. Lured by the scent
> Of steaming crowds, of rank disease, and death,
> Behold! he rushing cuts the briny flood,
> Swift as the Gale can bear the ship along;
> And, from the partners of that cruel trade,
> Which spoils unhappy Guinea of her sons,
> Demands his share of prey

Of the sharks found in West African waters, including great hammerheads and white sharks, two of the most common, tiger sharks and bull sharks, undertake long migrations and are likely to have followed ships laden with enslaved men, women and children for considerable distances. It is impossible today to know if they traversed the entire ocean or at a certain point turned back, relinquishing their place to deep-water predators such as blue, silky, shortfin and oceanic whitefin sharks, who would be joined by tiger and bull sharks from the West Atlantic as ships approached the American coast.

Whether or not shark migration patterns were changed by the trade as dramatically as human ones, what is certain from contemporary accounts, many of them written before the rise of the abolitionist movement by those engaged in slavery, is that sharks swarmed around slave ships and were used by their commanders to instil terror in both their human cargo and their potentially mutinous crew; and that large sharks followed slave ships into harbour, causing consternation among the locals. And of course, for those who survived the Middle Passage, there were plenty more sharks to be encountered on land.

I am pro-history, the prime minister said in a recent statement responding to the demands for the removal of statues that glorify colonialism and slavery, and I'm in favour of people understanding our past with all its imperfections . . .

Then his words took a strange swerve, conflating living people with statues, and history with the petty vanity of duplicitous politicians:

> I want to build people up, not tear people down. If we go around trying to Bowdlerise or edit our history in this way, it's like some politician sneakily trying to change his Wikipedia entry.

History, the argument seems to go, should be frozen at a certain point – one of the proponent's choosing – and not progress any further. Memorials erected to tyrants or exploiters, however vicious, must remain in place forever (unless they commemorate a ruler we have defeated in war, such as Saddam Hussain, traces of whom will be removed as speedily as possible). However, this model contradicts the evidence of history played out in the memorials we have erected in the past, a history which has always been fluid, ongoing. The Monument in London, erected in 1671 to commemorate the Great Fire of 1666, is a good example. The north panel carried a description of the conflagration that finished with the words:

On the third day, when it had now altogether vanquished all human counsel and resource, at the bidding, as we may well believe of heaven, the fatal fire stayed its course and everywhere died out.

In 1680, however, after the 'discovery' of a fictional Catholic plot, the Court of Common Council ordered that an inscription, in Latin and English, be fixed on the Monument, to make clear that:

the City of London was burnt and consumed with fire by the treachery and malice of the Papists in September in the year of Our Lord 1666.

To comply with this order the whole inscription had to be erased and re-carved to make room for a final, additional sentence:

But Popish frenzy, which wrought such horrors, is not yet quenched.

But the message of the Monument, though written in stone, was still not fixed. Shortly after James II came to the throne in 1685 the final sentence was removed, a decision that lasted only as long as his brief reign and was reversed by order of William III in 1689, when the calumny against the Catholics was reinstated, remaining enshrined in the heart of the City until it was finally removed in 1830. If it had not been, in those enlightened days, would the prime minister argue, as he did when discussing the taking down of statues on another occasion, that to remove such an accusation about a religious minority would be 'to lie about our history, and impoverish the education of generations to come'?

Generations to come are not in need of such concern; it is the present generation that is demanding its history be told, and taught, in full. Only then can the anger Darren spoke of be addressed.

VII

(JUST A) TIN CAN

To watch videos of events in Bristol, when the statue of slave trader Edward Colston was toppled, was to witness a compelling piece of theatre that compressed centuries of history into a few powerful moments. 'Pull It Down, Pull It Down!' chanted the crowds; when the statue pitched forward and landed on the ground, protesters put their feet on its neck and shouted, 'We Can't Breathe,' echoing the last words of Eric Garner, George Floyd and countless others who have died in police custody in North America in recent years, expressing perfectly through their action that this is not just a matter of twenty-first century police brutality but of a system that stretches back to the lifetime of the man on the plinth; a system that, watched by countless thousands around the world, they had symbolically overturned. (Which is why, it might be argued, the authorities who decided to press charges against those arrested for their involvement in events at the floating harbour might more usefully have proposed they be awarded honorary doctorates from the University of Bristol.) But this was not the end of the statue's journey.

It was really strange looking at Edward Colston's statue rolling down the street, John Akomfrah went on to say,

75

suddenly he was just a tin can. Because the work was being done while he was upright, in place, in situ. The minute he's dethroned, dislodged, he just becomes an object – suddenly the whole symbolic order disappeared.

Just a tin can. And then the final moment of poetic justice, when the owner of slave ships, over the sides of which so many men, women and children were cast, is himself thrown off the side of the dock and into the harbour from which his ships sailed forth, as the crowds cheer and a stream of bubbles breaks upon the surface of the green water. This viewer could only have felt greater satisfaction if a denizen of the deep, such as those lurking just beneath the surface of the boiling seas of JMW Turner's painting *The Slave Ship* (1840), originally entitled *Slavers Throwing Overboard the Dead and Dying – Typhoon Coming On*, had risen and swallowed the statue whole.

The historian I had met on the doorstep, I discovered, shared my delight.

I felt huge exhilaration,

she told me,

because I thought this is eighteenth century politics happening in front of my very eyes. It had that sense of an eighteenth century political riot – popular politics of the time was participation by riot – and so I felt I was watching a real historical moment. And for the first time it showed me that the dichotomy between we either have it up or we don't have it up, or we have it up with a little plaque about it, was wrong. You could do something like this and it would become part of another history. The argument has always been that somehow these statues would be thrown away. But now we've seen that you can put them in a museum – museums take things out of their context and put them into other contexts for people to learn from them. That's their job.

For her, events in Bristol took her back to the eighteenth century: they reminded me instead of the words of Frantz Fanon in *Black Skin, White Masks* (1952), who declared succinctly that 'we revolt simply because, for many reasons, we can no longer breathe.' The subsequent uprising, with its associated violence, brings about a 'collective catharsis' for colonial subjects when they find 'an outlet through which the forces accumulated in the form of aggression can be released'. If the camera footage is anything to go by, collective catharsis was much in evidence on the Bristol waterfront.

The historian has no time for the argument that the removal of statues is the erasure of history: instead, she told me, this is how history is made.

It's shocking to see the misapprehension of what all this is about.

Actually, I don't think these spokesmen are making a disingenuous political point; they literally *just don't understand.*

Perhaps, to help them along, they could be encouraged to read Rhodes' 'Confession of Faith', written in 1877:

I contend that we [the British] are the finest race in the world, and that the more of the world we inhabit the better it is for the human race. Just fancy those parts that are at present inhabited by the most despicable specimens of human beings what an alteration there would be if they were brought under Anglo-Saxon influence. [. . .] I contend that every acre added to our territory means in the future birth to some more of the English race who otherwise would not be brought into existence.

Africa is still lying ready for us it is our duty to take it. It is our duty to seize every opportunity of acquiring more territory and we should keep this one idea steadily before our eyes that more territory simply means more of the

Anglo-Saxon race more of the best the most human, most
honourable race the world possesses.

Some students of Rhodes' life might be tempted to excuse
the views expressed in the 'Confession of Faith' by pointing out that it was written in his early twenties, before he
matured into the philanthropist he later became. Others,
including the Chancellor of the University of Oxford, himself
the last colonial governor of Hong Kong, defend the statue
on the basis of the Rhodes Trust, which funds the studies of
twenty students from overseas, including five from Africa,
through the Mandela Rhodes Foundation. Nelson Mandela, the
Chancellor has pointed out, when setting up the scholarship,
looked up at a painting of Rhodes and said, 'Cecil, you and
I are going to have to work together.' If it was all right for
Mandela, the Chancellor argued, it was pretty well all right
for him. (Perhaps, it could be argued, after twenty-seven
years of imprisonment by an apartheid regime modelled on
Rhodes' racial views, from which he emerged to lead the
Rainbow Nation through its first years of independence,
Mandela had earned the right to make such a statement in a
way the Chancellor hadn't.) The person the current aims of
the Foundation might not be 'pretty all right' with is Rhodes
himself, whose intentions regarding the funds he intended
to leave were outlined in the codicil to his first will. (Written
before he had accumulated great wealth, he did not include
it in his final will.) They should be used, he explains:

To and for the establishment, promotion and development
of a Secret Society, the true aim and object whereof shall be
for the extension of British rule throughout the world [. . .]
and of colonisation by British subjects of all lands where
the means of livelihood are attainable by energy, labour

and enterprise, and especially the occupation by British settlers of the entire Continent of Africa, the Holy Land, the Valley of the Euphrates, the Islands of Cyprus and Canada, the whole of South America, the Islands of the Pacific not heretofore possessed by Great Britain, the whole of the Malay Archipelago, the seaboard of China and Japan, the ultimate recovery of the United States of America as an integral part of the British Empire [. . .] and, finally, the foundation of so great a Power as to render wars impossible and promote the best interests of humanity.

Perhaps the advent of such a utopia is what the statue is scanning the horizon for from its vantage point high above the street; its positioning, I heard on the Rhodes Must Fall demonstration on 16 June 2020, was based, at the advice of its subject, on the location of a statue of the Virgin Mary on the inner wall of the college quad, an in-joke making reference to something hidden from view to everyday passers-by on the High Street. What does the statue's continued presence mean to students who share identity with those Rhodes classified as 'despicable specimens of humanity'?

Temitope has Nigerian heritage and grew up in Italy before coming to the UK to study for his master's. He has been heavily involved in the Rhodes Must Fall campaign over the summer.

The first thing to say,

he tells me,

is that this is a continuing struggle – the media wants to paint it as a millennial thing or a new thing, but it isn't something that has just happened this summer or since the Rhodes Must Fall campaign began here in 2015 and 2016. You could say that people have wanted Rhodes to fall ever since the statue was first erected. This has been part of our public tradition. We often get the comeback that people at the time must have been OK with it, but that is not the case. We've published a lot of extracts from journals that were very critical of Rhodes during his lifetime and records of academics petitioning against the instalment of the statue on the facade. Power and money won over the voices of opposition and that is maybe the worst evil of it – it is not so much that it is an offence against personal sensibilities, it's that it represents disregard of people's voices. Wanting to take down statues is not a new process, it is still how public space unfolds, right?

He is right. In 1642, Parliamentarian soldiers occupying the city discharged muskets at the statue of the Virgin Mary on the front of the University Church that faces Rhodes in his eyrie on the other side of the High Street, dislodging the heads of both the Virgin and the child she is holding. For these revolutionary forces, religious imagery was oppressive, representing both heretical beliefs and the spiritual tyranny of Rome, as well as being a symbol, in the case of the University Church statue, of the rule of Charles I. Far from being a recent invention, arguments over statues have been a part of the politics of cities for centuries. How far did Temitope feel that the campaign had involved people in the community beyond the university?

It's an issue when it comes to protests,

he says,

because when you ask people here, women and men who have been activists in the city for decades, they know that at times they have collaborated with students on protests and then the students leave. They are investing energy in a drifting population. So at times there might be a feeling of suspicion or scepticism about getting involved in this protest with us students because we have so little stake in

26

Man & Van Services

Don'T
spreAD
coRONA

PLEASE TRY TO understand
that this is A Business
PLACE NOT A
social cLuB
we here To Make MoNEY

DO NOT
ENTER
without a
MASK

One Person at
A Time. Remember
to ware a mask
At all times in the
Shop. Thank you

One person
at a time. Ware
a Mask upon
entry.

CLOSED

This is A business
PLACE NOT
A social club
we're here To MAKE
A Living No TO hear
your Stories.
we have bills To
PAY DAHH
H.H.H.

ONE AT A
Time. No Mask.
No Service. Thank
you.

£45

LOVE YOU

HALT
DEINEN
TRAUM
ADLER SACH
2020

CHOOSE
LOVE

the city – individual students will leave in a year or two, so how much commitment can we give it?

This summer we were happy about the community's involvement, we were able to inspire, motivate and keep some of the townsfolk with us and give them a role in Rhodes Must Fall as much as possible during June, July and August. Now of course we are at a low point of energy after the high of the summer . . .

Had he been as inspired as many people were by the scenes on the waterfront in Bristol?

It was jubilance . . . a very happy moment. Only wicked people could see violence in it. That was not a violent mob, that was people taking charge and acting on their environment. It was a very democratic moment, I could say. That's what sprung us into action here. We said it has to be now. People will often give you a slippery-slope argument and say, if we accept what you're saying about this statue then we can't have any statues . . . I want to say, OK, that's fine, let's not have any statues! We have no bible that says we must have statues of anyone, right? There is a Facebook page called Conservatives Approaching the Point. When people say, 'If we agree with you, there are a lot of statues that should be taken down,' we say you're approaching the point. Yes!

Personally, I wonder if the politicians who oppose the removal of statues – whether on the facades of buildings, or, in the case of the likeness of slave owner Christopher Codrington, within the library he bequeathed to his old college – do so because it threatens their own status. They long to take their place in the pantheon of history but are aware their own cupboards are rattling with skeletons; they wake up at night remembering things they have written or said that could resurface on the web at any time, like scum rising in a pool. Will future generations judge them the way we now judge figures from the past? How can their own position be protected if Rhodes loses his?

Yes,

Temitope agrees,

and that also speaks to what donors feel when they threaten to pull the funding they have promised to the university if the statue is taken down. One of the arguments they make is that, if I give money, they promise me a plaque and then maybe in fifty years people say, let's take it down. Of course, no one is a saint – we might get to a point in the future where the discussion becomes more nuanced – and perhaps somewhere in the world a statue is being removed that might be worth more discussion; but Rhodes is not that difficult to judge, he is not in the middle!

One symbol of identity dominates the High Street; others appear in windows in other parts of the city. I knock at random at a door displaying a hand-drawn Black Lives Matter poster and ask the woman who opens it whether it felt important to her to put that message in her window during lockdown.

Yes, well, I'm American, as you can tell from my accent, she says.

I'm from Indiana originally. It was powerful learning about Breonna Taylor and George Floyd when you could see their pictures and you knew their families and it really connected with people. It's horrible, but as a white person a lot about racism was hidden from me in America along the way. The poster was a way to feel connected with what was going on in the world. I didn't feel comfortable going to a protest at the time . . . I didn't go to the Rhodes Must Fall march and I kind of wish I had, but this was the little thing I could do to be part of the movement without going down and being among a bunch of people. I chose to prioritise the Covid social distancing over protesting, but then was that the right move when social justice is so important? So I put up the sign and I've kept it up because I don't want it to fade from memory.

Another door, another poster, and this time a schoolgirl of around seventeen opens to me. Yes, she put the sign up in her bedroom window. She and people from the local community have been holding a weekly kneel, at the entrance to the park around the corner. It had been hard to keep it going with school starting again, not so many people were coming, but they will try to do it for as long as possible . . .

On the one hand, physically isolated from one another and spending more and more of our time on-screen, the pandemic might be the moment we would be expected to disembody completely and enter the digital future, electing avatars and algorithms to stand in for us. On the other, both the virus and shocking evidence of police brutality have reminded us that in the end we are indivisible from the physical world; we are bodies that need to breathe. For many, Covid is only one of the pandemics they live with in their lives; they also have to deal with what John Akomfrah has called 'a kind of death that hangs over black life'. Protest has been powerfully played out through symbolic physical gestures, as sportsmen knelt at the beginning of matches and the tennis champion Naomi Osaka was beamed across the world wearing a face mask naming a different victim of police brutality before every match. Many of us attending events will have knelt, or even just remained silent, for the amount of time Derek Chauvin kept his knee on George Floyd's neck, feeling the horror in our own bodies as seconds turned into minutes, into eight minutes forty-six seconds, in a way we never could by reading an account or even watching death arrive via a video.

A pebble-dashed house with exposed brickwork features in the upstairs window a sign that goes to the heart of things:

No one's free when others are oppressed

The woman who opens the door lives, she tells me, in a house of young professionals. She made the sign and put it up in her bedroom window. When I ask her whether she has been on any of the local Black Lives Matter or Rhodes Must Fall marches, her answer is as succinct as her poster.

Yes,

she says,

I think it is important to go on marches, but also to have a presence in your street.

Posters in the window, then, can both substitute for direct action and extend it, working to prevent a cause fading from public memory. Rebecca Solnit speaks to this in her foreword to Josh MacPhee's *Celebrate People's History: The Poster Book of Resistance and Revolution*: 'If revolutions often prompt posters to appear, the appearance of posters, murals and graffiti may foster revolution or at least breathe on the cinders, keeping the sparks alive until next time.'

And, as Temitope tells me:

What we are doing is the opposite of erasing history, it is bringing it up to the surface; bringing up a balanced view, including the voices of the vanquished. It is about the truth and it is about doing justice, at least now, to what happened. That is maybe what I care about the most. It's what links us to the struggles across the planet. We've received letters from small groups all over the world. One of the best was from a small town in Canada that has a school named after Cecil Rhodes and they have started the process of changing the name! So that's how far the impact of what is happening here has reached.

VIII

THE DISINGENUOUS SONG

I was haunted by the word the historian had used in her doorstep seminar on 'Rule Britannia' – the song, she said, had a 'disingenuous aporia', or philosophical paradox, at the heart of it: the determination not to become slaves alongside the equal determination to enslave others.

Here's a question: a song may come to represent a nation; can a nation resemble a song? Or to put it another way, does the aporia lie not only in the lyrics to 'Rule Britannia' but in Britannia herself? Is the ability to hold two conflicting views at the same time an essential part of being an English subject?

Those seeking answers to such questions need only follow the rainbows to an institution the pandemic has placed even more centrally in the nation's myth than it was before. In April, the week before Easter, as is traditional at the great festivals of the year, a mummers' play was staged that held the country riveted to its nightly updates. The man who himself, through the office conferred upon him by the people, represented the nation, grew sick with the virus. (The theory that this was all an elaborate piece of stagecraft designed to garner the sympathy and acquiescence of the public, and that in fact he was perfectly well, convinced only a small number.) For some at least, this figure – stout, tousle-headed, unpredictable and known universally by his Christian name, like a family pet – was a British bulldog, caught in a soap opera that had taken a nasty turn. Once he passed through the hospital gates to spend three days on an intensive care ward, the pleasures of schadenfreude swiftly curdled and even his sworn enemies expressed sympathy. Would he emerge again, bluster and prevarication intact?

When he did, via video, it was on Easter Sunday, as though he had taken the sickness of the nation upon himself, passed through the valley of death and risen again. (Or did he appear as a stand-in for the Easter bunny, whose absence had been mourned by so many children around the world?) In any case, as he was fully aware, he was a totem object, newly clothed in symbolism. This was his resurrection speech, baby, aimed at disciples and naysayers alike. He lost no time in making a moving tribute to those he had encountered on his journey from the jaws of death back to our screens. The NHS was, he told us, 'our greatest national asset'. It had saved his life, 'no question', and it was 'hard to find the words to express [his] debt'. He had, over the last seven days, seen the pressure the service was under and it had clearly come as a revelation. He reeled off a list of the kind of workers present in a hospital, all of whom had 'kept coming to work, kept putting themselves in harm's way, kept risking this deadly virus', particularly as the government had not provided them with the necessary personal protective equipment. He went on to thank the doctors, 'men and women but several of them for some reason called Nick', who took crucial decisions for which he would remain grateful for the rest of his life, and singled out two nurses in particular 'who stood by my bedside for forty-eight hours when things could have gone either way. They are Jenny from New Zealand – Invercargill on the South

Island to be exact – and Luis from Portugal – near Porto.' In an accurate description of the working life of a nurse, he told us how 'every second of the night they were watching and they were thinking and they were caring and making the interventions I needed'.

Finally, he told us, 'We will win because our NHS is the beating heart of this country. It is the best of this country. It is unconquerable. It is powered by love.' He allowed himself a moment of visible emotion during which the nation wondered if he was going to shed a tear or two before doing what he would doubtless call 'manning up' and signing off with a government slogan.

So why was this piece of theatre as riddled with paradox as a Swiss cheese is with holes? In 2019, the year our actor was elected, his party had been in government for nine years. Waiting lists in the NHS were at record highs, cancer patients weren't getting treatment on time, nursing bursaries had been cut and there was a shortage of almost 43,000 nurses. 'Our greatest national asset' was bleeding staff at every level, exhausted and disheartened, with thousands returning to EU countries before their right to travel and work freely in the UK was removed. (It is not recorded whether 'Luis from Portugal' has joined them.) Perhaps the achievement that best exemplifies the Conservatives' approach was the sale of the NHS-owned blood plasma company for around £230m to the private equity firm Bain Capital in 2013; Bain Capital in turn sold it on for a sum approaching £820m to a Chinese company three years later. The 'beating heart of this country' must pay if it wants to keep pumping.

The aporia in the televised address was present also in the praise given to those who had saved its maker's life. Their work might make them 'heroes', in the language of a mummers' play; but they would still have to pay to park their cars at the hospitals they drove to in an effort to stay safe and avoid public transport. What is more, if they had responded to recruitment drives and come from certain territories overseas, as many had done, they would have to pay to access NHS services when they themselves got sick. Finally, if they came from Europe they would now have to fill in interminable forms and wait for extended periods to learn whether they had a right to continue living here at all. Heroes, in other words, are both temporary and disposable.

But this has always been the case. In 1948, when the National Health Service was set up, there was also a shortage of nursing staff, of 48,000, a mere 5,000 more than the short-fall in numbers today. A recruitment drive was started in the West Indies: members of the so-called Windrush Generation were promised a new life of opportunity in the mother country and answered the call, along with those who came to drive buses and trains and work in factories and industry. When their services were no longer required, these heroes of post-war reconstruction were told they were perhaps not so British after all. Several who had arrived with their parents as young children and paid tax in the UK all their working lives found themselves sent back to countries they did not know.

'After ten years of cuts we are on our knees already,' an accident and emergency nurse told me at the beginning of the pandemic, when she was redeployed to a Covid ward. 'Telling the public that the Health Service is fully equipped and prepared' – something the government was constantly doing at the beginning of the pandemic – 'is essentially a lie.'

The dissonance in the mummers' play between flowery locution and murderous intent is deliberate, part of the drama: fete the thing you will destroy. Suddenly the rainbow flag transforms into a matador's cape, unfurled and flapped in the face of the public to distract attention from the sword going in, finding its way inexorably between muscle and bone to the heart.

IX

NO MORE ISLANDS

'There are no more deserts, there are no more islands,' wrote Albert Camus in 'The Minotaur, or The Halt at Oran'.

> Yet the need for them makes itself felt. If we are to understand the world, we must turn aside from it; if we are to serve men better, we must briefly hold them at a distance. But where are we to find the solitude necessary to strength, the long breathing space in which the mind can gather itself together and courage take stock of itself?

How surprised the author of *The Plague* would have been if he had known that the distance he craved would be delivered by a virus – and that the same virus would return his novel to the bestseller lists, more than seventy years after it was written. Solitude ceased to be a scarce commodity when apartments became as isolated as atolls, houses as mountaintops. Here, at least for those lucky enough to be furloughed from their jobs, was the long breathing space of which Camus had written and of which they had only dreamt, an opportunity to pursue a thousand projects long put on hold.

Yet it was hard to bring those projects into focus. The extraordinary events unfolding across the world kept us rooted in the present, anchored to the next news report, alternately stupefied and enraged by the antics of our supposed leaders and their inability to rise to the crisis. On social media platforms, writers, to take one example, either mourned their inability to write or comforted each other that to be unable to write in such a situation was perfectly normal. Meanwhile the rest of the world was writing feverishly, or attacking what others had written, the air full of words ricocheting from platform to platform, from one phone to the next. For those accustomed to generating material by moving through space – who could, in the loosest possible terms, and bearing fully in mind all the reservations we now have about long-distance travel, be classified as travel writers – to be confined was doubly frustrating. As the narrator of Olga Tokarczuk's *Flights* tells her readers:

> I'm simply not in possession of the vegetable capacity. I can't extract nutrition from the ground, I am the anti-Antaeus. My energy derives from movement – from the shuddering of buses, the rumble of planes, trains' and ferries' rocking.

Instead, time yawned ahead with none of the energy of movement even to and from work and no one to report to but ourselves. And what was that particular boss saying? *If you don't realise the projects you have put off for so long because you didn't have time to complete them now, when you have all the time in the world, who are you kidding?*

At the same time, I was aware equally of how lucky I was in being able to work from home and of the marginal nature of the contribution I was making at this time of crisis, compared to those putting their lives at risk to serve others. It seems I wasn't alone in feeling this vague unease.

Attracted by a rainbow poster in a window, I ring the bell.
A young girl appears behind the glass but signals vigorously
that she isn't going to open the door, or even the window – at
least that's what I think she is trying to communicate through
our exchanges in an improvised sign language, but she also
seems to be pointing to the side of the house where there
is an alley, through which after a minute or two her father
emerges to see what is going on. I ask him about the poster,
which it turns out has been made by the artist observing
us as we speak, and also whether he has taken part in the
clapping for the NHS.

Every Thursday between half and two-thirds of the people
on the street were clapping,

he tells me.

It was a nice way to see everybody else's faces, because
of course everyone was in complete lockdown – it was a
way of connecting for a moment or two on a Thursday
night, that was a big part of it. Yeah, I found it moving,
particularly at the beginning, because of course there were
lots of people in a very bad way and the images on the
TV and so on were very harrowing. We've not had to put
ourselves through any of that; we've been pretty safe, able
to stay isolated, so I think there's a little bit of guilt there
as well . . . Because we're able to work from home and so
on but other people haven't had that choice, so there's a
sense of wanting to show appreciation for the NHS, but
there's also a feeling of guilt.

A feeling of guilt: not something advertised in windows,
but present nonetheless, and only assuaged through the
display of slogans and in communal rituals.

For others, lockdown was a time to rethink their working
practice. Many swore, after they had enjoyed spending more
time at home with their partners and children, that they

93

would never go back to travelling every day to work in an office but would continue working *remotely*, which meant closer to those they cared about. They were more productive this way, they explained, as long as their partner continued to manage the bulk of the childcare. Usually those confident enough to make such statements were also those sure their job would not be one trimmed in the swingeing economies that were surely coming. For those who had never experienced the stability of the nine-to-five life or had long ago exchanged it for the precarious freedoms and pleasures of self-employment, there was a certain irony to this: what, they get our lifestyle and keep their money and job security? No one offered us that deal! But when the first wave of redundancies breaks upon the shoreline they fall silent, quietly telling themselves just maybe they'd made the right choice after all.

In the middle of lockdown I had the reverse experience. A headhunter got in touch dangling the possibility of a job that would have taken all my resources and energy but been rewarding and fascinating. I asked for time to think about it. Lone creatives often have a surfeit of the solitude Camus craved, even more so when a virus means it is at first not possible and later not desirable to work at cafe tables surrounded by the hum of conversation, or in libraries by the lack of it; returning to the centre of things had its appeal. But what about this idea, or that project, which would subsequently never be realised? What of them? In such situations, when difficult decisions are necessary, mankind has often relied on the rule of chance. My eyes wandered up to a shelf where I saw a copy of *The Sayings of Confucius* in a 1955 paperback edition published by the New American Library for 50 cents. I'd picked it up a few months earlier on a market stall but scarcely glanced inside. Now I took it down and opened it at random, seeking guidance. 'A man's knowledge may be sufficient for a post but his superiority insufficient for maintaining it,' I read on the first page my eyes alighted on,

> so although he gets the post he is sure to lose it.
>
> Both knowledge and superiority may be sufficient, but if he administers it without dignity the people will not be respectful.
>
> Both knowledge and superiority may be sufficient, and he may administer it with dignity, but if he acts contrary to the rites, he is not yet competent.

Regarding the knowledge required I felt fairly secure. Dignity, not so much. Superiority is for others to assess. But it was those rites of which the sage speaks that were the clincher: I've never had those down. Ridiculous, you're thinking, to base a life decision on a random quotation; but the airwaves daily delivered far more ridiculous decisions made by those supposedly steering us through the crisis. In the circumstances, chance seemed as good a steer as any.

X

NOTHING TO LOSE
BUT YOUR FOOD CHAINS

The challenges since the arrival of Covid faced by those who tap keyboards for a living have been much reported in the press, but they are not even half the story. We are, as the virus has reminded us, despite all our efforts to outsource ourselves through screens, algorithms and avatars, just bodies, and bodies must be fed. Someone had to feed us when the world shut down, and they did – from those working for vast agri-businesses, picking and packing fruit and vegetables, to those in food processing plants or in haulage, driving the delivery trucks that bring food to market, right down to the small businesses supplying their local neighbourhoods with food. For these people there was no isolation at home, no furlough; work continued and it was harder than ever. And although arguably the crisis has brought slightly greater understanding of the value of the role they perform – evidenced by the shout-outs in windows to Key Workers, Essential Workers, Front-Line Workers, Delivery Drivers – their activity remains largely invisible, drowned in the shadows extending beyond the warm glow of our national love for the NHS.

How was it for them, I wondered. My investigation began at the micro-end of the scale with a couple who run a bakery

and cafe – she in charge of the baking operation and he the
front of house – supported by a team of three. I join them
over their half-hour lunch break, one or another of the team
regularly getting up when an alarm pings out the back to say
something needs taking out or adjusting. To hear them talk
of the early days of lockdown is a little like hearing people
speak of the outbreak of a war.

There was that day they announced the pubs and restaurants were closing,

the baker says,

and we were thinking, that's it, we'll have to close; but
then I thought, sure, we'll have to shut the cafe, but if
Sainsbury's is still open then I can make bread, because
it's a food product.

– My instinct when lockdown happened was to close,
her partner says.

She shakes her head.

I'd go crazy if I wasn't working, but I think you'd rather
enjoy it!

– Yes,

he says,

I'm a natural furlough kind of a guy!

But when the laughter has died down, he turns serious
again.

At various points I wasn't sure whether what we were
doing was officially sanctioned or not, because it wasn't
very clear. We thought we'd stay open for the people who
depend on us, the community aspect of it.

Did you feel a sense of a duty to do that, I ask them.

In a way yes,

the baker says,

because a lot of our customers are a bit older ... That's the
amazing thing about bread, you see the same people week

in and week out. He – nodding at her partner – is the key contact person in their day for quite a few people, I think.

I remember at lockdown seeing a queue right down the street to the bakery door – it looked like something from the Great Depression, with better clothes and social distancing. Was it stressful?

On some levels it was less stressful because we thought, right, shut down the cafe, make an absolute mother lode of bread. We'll slim down the number of breads we do, just hone in our focus, get really efficient and we'll fly like that. For me it was probably one of the most rewarding periods of work I ever had, I really enjoyed it.

– Knowing every day that we were going to sell everything was very energising,

he says.

We made as much bread each day as we possibly could, and it sold out in four hours. It felt like we didn't suffer any of the strange effects lots of other people did during lockdown. I continued to see hundreds of people every day in the shop – albeit not for long conversations.

– There was a moment when I was like, oh my God, how much bread am I going to be having to make here, she says.

I'm making as much as I can and still he's having to walk down the queue and tell people we haven't got bread for them. It was tiring, longer days, having to mentally prepare for this running out or that running out and maybe not being able to get hold of it.

That must have been difficult . . . a lot of ingredients disappeared from the shelves back in March.

You know when there was that flour shortage, he says,

people were begging us for flour.

– We were really lucky,

she says,

well, a mixture of luck and an instance of your ideology having knock-on benefits. Because we deal directly with the farmers selling grain, we have tons and tons of grain in storage in silos at the mill . . .

– Most bakers would buy flour from a mill,

her partner adds,

but we buy grain, pay for it to be transported to the mill and then pay for the miller to mill it and transport it to us, as and when we need. We've got two silos at the mill filled with our grain.

– But the reason we did that is we want to know where the grain came from,

she explains,

working directly with the farmers and having a relation-ship with the people who are growing our wheat. We're sourdough, so we don't need yeast. On the pastries side, our dry goods supplier, who is a big organic wholesaler and who we get chocolate, dried fruit and unrefined sugar from, completely shut down and didn't reopen for several months. So every Monday morning I was scrabbling around on the internet to try and find supplies.

– In a sense everything stayed the same,

her partner says.

I mean quite a few days a week we get up very early – about half three or three forty-five in the morning – so when you finish work you're thinking about getting to bed as quickly as possible, making sure you don't eat too late, you don't have coffee too late, don't get overexcited, that you get off your phone after such-and-such a time; as it went on I became more conscious of the need to be absolutely disciplined about that.

— Yes, I felt this is what I have to do for this time,
she says,
my responsibility is to stay healthy so I can work, and
that's going to be my life for a while . . .
— Her life was working, sleeping, going for a run, doing
a bit of yoga and that was it,
he says, to laughter from the rest of the team.
— What do you mean, it's still my life now,
she replies.
Did their relationship with their customers change?
Once we set up our online ordering system,
he explains,
orders were flooding in and the warmth and gratitude from
the people who made the trip to pick them up was energising and encouraging. Where there was a little space for
people to leave a comment by their order they wrote things
like 'keep going, thank you so much, it's the highlight
of our week'. It was so nice to have that happening and
for sales to be up 40 per cent pretty much overnight. We
started doing veg boxes and selling more cheese, adding
salami, milk and yoghurt . . . We went from selling sixty
cartons to two hundred cartons of eggs a week.
I can't help being conscious as he speaks of the contrast
between their experience and of others I know in the neighbourhood running their own businesses who wonder daily if
they can survive. This might sound like a strange question,
I ask, but did it ever feel odd that the bakery was thriving
while others around you were in such difficulties?
Definitely,
she says.
We're both hospitality lifers, we've got so many friends
in the industry, so many who run their own businesses.
Bakers were all doing well, but a good friend of mine and

a couple of his have restaurants and they were just . . . we felt it keenly for them. It contributed to the feeling we had of being unbelievably fortunate . . . that we'd been open long enough to establish a customer base and that our core product is a staple food.

– And that we weren't in the city centre,

he adds,

that we were in a neighbourhood where a lot of people were working from home and eating at home. What else were they going to spend their food money on?

Working in an artisanal business like this, which controls every aspect of its production chain and sells its product to a relatively affluent clientele, is as far from the experience of working in the large-scale globalised food industry as it is possible to imagine. Ten minutes or so on foot from the bakery there is a house with a front window I have only ever seen decorated with a poster when there is an election approaching. Behind the door lives a researcher for a union that represents workers across the food sector, from field to forecourt, as she puts it. I ask her what issues she had come across.

There was a divide between blue-collar and white-collar experience,

she tells me.

The terms seem old-fashioned, but it works as a way of looking at lockdown. You remember when the government said, 'If you can work at home, work at home'? Well, by definition, if you are in any kind of manufacturing, on a production line or on the shop floor, you can't work at home. One of the interesting things that was happening at some food manufacturers was that because the HR people and the senior managers and some of the junior managers could work from home they did, while the production line workers were coming across all sorts of problems connected with Covid on the production line – for example, the proximity, the closeness of working together rather than there being any social distancing – but when they raised this the managers weren't there to see what they were talking about: they were either at home or carefully isolated in offices and didn't go onto the line to see for themselves what was happening, so they didn't believe what people were saying.

Were there clear directions issued for those operating such businesses?

At the beginning, nobody knew what to do at any level – government, employers, unions – and in that vacuum an awful lot of anxiety and fear grew. And although some employers responded very well and went above and beyond the government guidance because they could see it didn't go far enough, the thing I've had people raising in phone calls with us is that it was profit before people, particularly in the food sector because it's quite cut-throat and the profit margins are very slim.

So it was a strange situation for many people, where outside the workplace you could be fined for not social distancing but as soon as you clocked on you were in a different world where suddenly it didn't matter, just so long as the volume of production was kept up and the supermarkets kept their shelves full. That caused untold stress and anxiety and it did lead to people walking off the job and sites having to close because people were so terrified about what they were being asked to do.

Many of those people were going into work and then going home to a household where they might have an elderly relative with underlying conditions, or they might have a child with asthma or a partner who was undergoing chemotherapy – all those kind of personal situations that made it even worse. If they developed symptoms, better employers had them stay at home on 80 per cent pay, but the worse employers, and this was very frequently told to us, they were just put on statutory sick pay, that's around £95 a week; for some people their rent was £90 a week so they were being left with £5 a week to live on. One of the early fatalities from Covid was a woman working in a meat-processing factory. She couldn't live on her sick pay, so she went back to work even though she had symptoms and eventually she died. If that employer had told her to stay at home on 80 per cent of her pay she wouldn't have been transmitting the disease, and she also would probably have survived.

These workers are the people producing the products for supermarket shelves. Others have to stack those shelves and operate the tills. What was life like for them during the lockdown?

This is important,

she says,

because the experience of people working in supermarkets hasn't really come out. Things have calmed down a bit now but in the early weeks and months there were a lot of tears, union reps told me, and a huge amount of anxiety for staff – because of the uncertainty, because they were dealing with people panic-buying, because managers in some cases were keeping themselves safe by isolating in a back office, rather than being on the shop floor helping and providing support. A socially distanced queue would form outside the doors but once customers were in the shop, customers would get very close to members of staff or even tap them on the shoulder to get their attention, and this is at a time when people were supposed to be two metres apart. All the pressures they normally faced at work were multiplied by Covid and it became hugely stressful. It can be quite an abusive environment and Covid made that worse, at least in the early stages. Supermarket staff were asked to take on customers' anger, stress and anxiety at a time when they would have already been feeling anxious themselves, under pressure to keep the whole operation going and the shelves stacked.

The products produced on production lines like the ones she is describing are very different from those originating at the other end of the scale, in a business like the bakery. What can she tell me of their story?

It's mind-boggling! The framing of food in supermarkets is all about it being fresh – they increasingly use pictures of farmers and say they have strong relationships with suppliers, carrying on the illusion the food is all hand-produced, not that far from where the consumer lives. Most of the time customers going into a supermarket pick up a chicken and leek pie and never wonder where the leek in it came from and how many people have been involved in getting it from the field into the pie, how many stages it has gone through – but it will have travelled all over the place. A pie like that represents a relatively low level of processing. If you take something like instant noodles, the flavouring that goes on top is dehydrated – a long way from originally being an onion or something! One brand of noodles starts off at a plant in the south-west of the UK but it travels to Germany to have its toppings put on: this is a global company that has different divisions and their toppings division is in Germany; then it travels back to the UK to be finished, packaged and have the lid put on. There are even perishable foods that travel halfway around the world to have just one aspect of the production done to them. For example, prawns that are part of a fish-processing company in Scotland are sent to Thailand to have their shells removed, the thinking being that Thai people are more manually dextrous – and you can also pay them less! Then the shelled prawns are brought back to Scotland to be put in a fish pie or whatever.

That's the long-shot view, ranging across countries and continents, just as the industry itself does. But now we zoom in once more, back to the level of human experience. I finally find a time when a friend who works shifts in a supermarket can meet up and tell me how it was for him, going to work when the world was locked down.

It's a very complicated subject,

he says.

It was a mix of positive and negative. Positive because in a very scary moment you are part of doing something to help society, to help your community to go forward, not give up. At least that was a positive feeling. Negative because you could be a victim.

I caught the virus. I was really sick.

When the virus started, to be honest, nobody was prepared for it. We didn't have hand gel, we didn't have masks, we didn't have gloves, we didn't have screens at the tills for at least, if I am not wrong, two months. They brought these things much later. I was thinking that the government would announce the two-metre distance rule. But they didn't require it for us because, doing customer service, I have to be close enough to take a card from the customer, to take cash, to give change – the distance between a customer and me is only –

he holds out his arm –

half a metre. That situation, if they had taken proper responsibility it would have been better than it is. But

I think these companies care more about money than their employees.

Did they give you any advice or instructions?

No. No, no, no, not at all. Just to keep running the business, that's it. We just came to work, went home. They didn't care to sit and have a meeting for ten or fifteen minutes to discuss what we have to do, how to behave. About two months later they bring hand gel and gloves, very, very late. There were more jobs we had to do because it was getting very busy, the restaurants were closed, takeaway was closed, people were coming to buy food and cook at home so we worked very hard. We expected some more money, a bonus, but they didn't do that. For one month they gave us a sandwich free for lunch but after one month they stopped it.

A sandwich instead of a bonus: I suppose that must be what they call a meal deal. I wanted to ask, did you find people were more aggressive because of the situation, or when stock ran out?

To be honest, people looked very down, not aggressive, more anxious, worried. There were very few incidents. Often there was a queue of thirty people standing outside and they restricted how many people could come in. I was getting very upset about how long people had to wait outside just to buy a sandwich and I was asking the manager, please could you provide more till operators – I don't blame the manager, it's the company that has cut staff to make more money. We ran out of many things – toilet paper, flour, eggs . . .

I see older people who are coming in with no one to help them and sometimes I help them – they are lovely sweet people, regular customers. I can see lots of stress on the people who come in. They used to come and talk to each other, shake hands, now they avoid talking to each other, they just take care of themselves. The side effects are anxiety, stress and depression. People losing their lives is one side, but mental health is going to be badly affected. People are even scared to go and see their own family. Loneliness is a big, big challenge for older people. People's behaviour is changed because they are very worried.

This is a man who has travelled across the world, a journey of unimaginable difficulty, terror and peril, to share his wisdom and compassion from behind the till. I come across an extraordinary contrast in attitude when an opportunity arises for my partner and me to slip out of the city and spend a weekend cycling along the coast. Simply to be somewhere different, after months of lockdown, is as intoxicating as the sea air we gulp greedily into our lungs; but even here I am scanning windows. In a small, run-down resort we come across a shopfront which is full of signs, communicating with potential customers before they enter the premises. Among the multiple messages taped to the glass are these words:

ONE PERSON
AT A TIME. WARE
A MASK UPON
ENTRY.

We're here to MAKE
A LIVING NO TO HeAR
YOUR sTories.

PLEASE TRY TO unDERstAND
that this is A Business
PlACE NOT A
SOCIAL CLUB
WE here to Make MONEY

We have biLLs TO
PAY. DAAHH

The union researcher had told me of the aggression directed towards staff on the shop floor by customers that has been exacerbated by the crisis. In this case, in a pre-emptive strike that may be prompted by genuine fear, it is directed towards the customer before they have entered the premises.

To be honest there are always aggressive people when you are in customer service,

my friend explains.

I don't blame them because some of them may be homeless, some of them may be jobless, some of them may have depression and anxiety. When they are coming to you, you are the victim, you have to ignore your rights and do something to sort out the situation. In customer service you have to deal with this, you have to be a doctor, you have to be a psychologist. Their stress is coming on you at the end of the day when you finish your shift. It's a difficult job.

How did you realise you'd caught the virus, I ask.

Sunday was my day off, I asked my wife to go for a walk, he says.

After ten or fifteen minutes I feel very weak, I ask my wife to sit, I sit by the river and I was thinking something strange is happening. I go home and I couldn't stop coughing, I had a high fever, no sleep, very weak. For two weeks I was locked down and after that my holiday started which I had booked before that and I had to use that to get better. No holiday for me now till next year, I have to keep working continuously; I spent my holiday when I was sick! If they had provided hand gel and screens earlier it would have been much better.

When I got back the manager didn't even ask me how I was, can you believe it, they were just ignoring me, and I've been working there for many years. I wondered, am

I human? I know I'm doing a good job . . . But they are gossiping behind you, saying, oh he just made it up, he didn't have the virus, he just wanted to have time off . . . But I was seriously ill, honestly, I couldn't even sit on my bed. Thousands of jobs are lost. When companies know there's not enough jobs they take more advantage of you – for example, we used to be paid for a half-hour break but they don't pay it now. They took it away. The bank holiday used to be paid double, they made it time-and-a-half, now it is normal pay. Sunday is normal pay, midnight is normal pay. These are the bad changes that are happening and the cost of living is going up, up, up. More work, less pay, too much pressure, this is the biggest challenge for human beings coming out of Covid-19, because companies are taking advantage because of it. You are the loser and they are the winner.

XI

JUST ASK ME QUESTIONS

We've arranged to meet at the pub, and I turn up at 9.30 in the morning on the dot as instructed but the front door is still locked. During the second lockdown the pub has run a small shop and offered a food takeaway service from its premises, but during the first it remained dark and I'm keen to hear what impact this had on its owners. As I turn the corner I hear someone call my name: the landlady is walking down the street towards me flanked by two of her staff, triggering an image in my mind not unlike a scene from an old movie of a gangland boss pacing out her territory. And why not? Through hard work, creativity and sheer force of personality combined with her husband's skill in the kitchen, she has stamped her identity on this neighbourhood, shifting the ambiance of its streets for ever.

OK, I've got ten minutes,
she tells me as we walk together through the back door.
Hello darlings,
she calls to the staff in the kitchen where the lights are already on.
Make a coffee for the cooks,
she says to the man at her elbow,
and a cappuccino for James here.

She pulls a chair out at a table and I sit down opposite her.
Right,

she says.

Just ask me questions, dude.

What are your memories of that first lockdown, when the
pub had to close, I ask.

My husband had been talking about this Covid thing since
December when he first saw it on the news; he said, this
is problematic and I was (sarcastically), oh yeah? And he
said, no, this *is* problematic, it's heading our way. When
it hit the UK in March and it was announced we'd have
to close, I was hysterical really. I wasn't here on the last
night, I walked out crying about five o'clock on the Friday
afternoon. We shut that Saturday. It was Mother's Day
weekend, the biggest weekend for us since Christmas.
All the fridges were full, we were loaded up with pro-
duce, beer and booze. Forget Covid, we had thousands of
pounds of losses on that first weekend: losses in takings,
plus losses in stock and all kinds of waste; I'm still sorting
out credits now, months later. My office is a mess, I'm
searching out credit notes so I can speak to people and to
my bookkeeper – it's hell to be honest. We didn't want to
come back into this building until we had money in the
bank – we were so scared we wouldn't have the money
to buy from suppliers.

Were you able to get business support under the schemes
the government set up?

We weren't eligible for any grants or help from anybody
because our rateable value was too high and the only
businesses the government was going to give aid to in this
sector were those with a rateable value of up to £50,000.
We don't decide our rateable value, it's decided by the
council and it's based on your rent and your earnings.

Our rents are enormous because we're with the brewery and yes, we are taking money in this establishment, but I always say, why should you be a victim of your success? Just because we're taking money it doesn't mean we're super-loaded – we bloody work hard, and we've been able to pay ourselves and not get into debt and run this business for eleven years. Because of that our rateable value is higher, so we lose out.

Did you feel an added weight of responsibility because of the people you employ, I ask.

Yeah, because everybody else was doing takeaway apart from us. We started doing takeaway that first weekend, but straightaway one of our staff went down with Covid, so we had to close for two weeks and that stopped it all. We would probably have carried on right through the first lockdown, but the motivation went in that two weeks. We were too scared to start up again until we had money in the bank – we had to get a big bank overdraft overnight. So there was a lot of pressure. I felt really guilty. Our business partner was saying, come on guys, you can do it, but I was saying, I can't, I can't. But this (second) lockdown there was no way we were stopping. In one day, we turned the pub around into a shop and just got on with it.

I suppose the pressure didn't stop with work, I suggest – you've got young children as well. It often falls to women who are working to supervise homeschooling. How did that go?

She laughs shortly.

It was a disaster really. I went into some sort of meltdown. I had to see my doctor at the end of the summer and have some help with my anxiety. I only did about two weeks' homeschooling because I couldn't stop thinking about the pub, I couldn't concentrate. In the end I told the school it wouldn't happen, we wouldn't be doing any homeschooling. They took the children on as key-worker children because the pub had done so much in the past few years supporting the school financially and in other ways.

We're interrupted by her phone. She's been out running already after dropping off the children at school and had intended to meet up with a running partner but had missed her in the autumnal mist that has risen from the river and enveloped the streets this morning. Has running helped during lockdown, I ask when she ends the call.

I do Joe Wicks or I run and at the moment I'm running. Joe Wicks was amazing during lockdown. Then one day I took the puppy for a walk and I was running up to this group of mums from school with their dogs who I hadn't seen for ages and I was really excited about Joe Wicks, I was thinking, I can't wait to do a burpee in front of you, but I had to rescue the puppy from being attacked by a bigger dog because he was nipping her. I ran to pick her up like a football, like I was a goalie, and I slipped and landed on my knee and I couldn't walk properly for *nearly four months*. I had to go to hospital and have an X-ray. That ruined my lockdown, I never did any exercise after that until very recently. Yeah, it was rubbish. I was really upset about that.

I'm thinking you've had about twenty-five years' bad luck in one year, I say.

The only good luck was having more time with the kids. All those half-terms we've missed because of work! I always tell my staff they can't book holidays in half-term and then what do they do? For that, and for the puppy, lockdown was amazing. My husband was relaxed, and when he's happy, I'm super-happy. Watching him under pressure is quite stressful – well, us watching each other. He hasn't been dealing with the stress as well as I have, really, but then the doctor helped me with my stress!

She's been looking away from me, towards the front door, as she speaks and she suddenly shouts:

Hey! What's he doing?

and she's on her feet, running towards the back of the building. It turns out someone is parking a van in front of the bins that are due to be collected this morning – the mystery is how she's seen it from where we're sitting. A member of staff who is quietly working at a neighbouring table smiles at my bafflement.

– She saw it in the mirror,

he says.

– She doesn't miss much,

someone else says as he walks past.

Out the back I can hear her issuing instructions to give mince pies and coffee to the bin men:

They're the most important people to the business,

she's telling somebody,

you have to keep the bin men happy.

Momentum is building, opening time for the shop is getting nearer and when she rejoins me, I know our time together is drawing to a close. I ask her whether she thinks we will ever go back to how it was before.

I think people will be more wary,

she says.

We were watching something last night, *DIY SOS*, that was filmed before all this happened and the presenter took a bite out of a pasty and then gave it to one of the builders and we were all thinking you wouldn't do that now. I don't think there'll be so much hugging anymore and I'm the most tactile person out. I used to hug my customers! But it is what it is. If we lose the business, we lose the business; I don't think we're out of the woods. If we go into another lockdown after Christmas we'll be going into tricky land.

What are they going to do on New Year's Eve, shut pubs at ten? That's a joke.

Even my daughter said to me this morning, what, does that mean coronavirus is going to go away for one day at Christmas, Mum? And she's seven.

And I said, no, you're right, it's not going to just disappear.

Many businesses, on the other hand, will do just that; but something tells me this won't be one of them.

XII

THE FLOATING PHILOSOPHER

I'm down by the river again, on the towpath that became a kind of superhighway during lockdown for people seeking fresh air during the hour a day they were allowed to leave their dwellings for exercise: walkers, joggers, cyclists, dogs, squeezed together into the narrow space, weaving in and out of each other at different speeds, creating a melee along the narrow strip between the path's edge and the water. We were regulars as the evenings got longer, enjoying with hundreds of others the signs of the seasons shifting; the luminous strands of willow coming into leaf and dangling just above the river surface, a stately flotilla of eight white geese escorting four chicks, the motionless heron standing sentry-duty at the other bank, candyfloss-white blossoms of horse chestnut flecked with pink and yellow. The riverbank along this stretch is crowded with houseboats, ranging from immaculate, seaworthy barges and flashy motor cruisers to craft that look in danger of capsizing in the shallowest waters, their peeling paint revealing porous, flaky woodwork, their decks crowded with rubbish and windows partially obscured with random scraps of cloth. A sign went up during lockdown, reminding strollers that the boats were people's homes and that several boat-dwellers were isolating, suggesting walkers

116

diverted through adjoining fields to give them some space, but the number of people using the path continued to grow as spring moved into summer.

The resident of one boat at least appears unconcerned to be joined by so many land-dwellers: instead he is determined to communicate with them. The windows on a narrowboat are low and small, unsuitable for the display of posters or banners; instead, early on in lockdown, the entire land-facing side of this particular boat was covered in handwritten signs taped to its surface. The signs were compressed, eloquent and informative, fuelled, the reader sensed, by an anger that would not be easily deflected. One compared deaths in the UK from Covid with those in China and Vietnam, with figures updated on a weekly basis. An image still on my phone has the notice stating:

> CHINA COVID DEATHS
> (with zero warning)
> 4,634

> UK COVID DEATHS
> (with 3 months warning)
> 41,369

> VIETNAM COVID DEATHS
> (with 3 months warning)
> 24

Another demands:

> LET GPs TEST 4 COVID!
> END THE RECKLESS HEALTH
> PRIVATISATION EXPERIMENT!
> SMASHING CIVIL LIBERTIES
> WILL NOT CONTROL THE VIRUS!

I kept an eye on the boat over the weeks and months but it wasn't until summer was shifting into autumn that I happened to pass when its resident was on deck and we could speak. He invites me on board and we sit in the narrow, vaulted wooden space, me next to the open door, to talk.

Was it the fact there were so many people on the towpath during lockdown that gave you the idea to use the side of the boat as a billboard, I ask.

Yes, partly. It was so busy along here I thought I should use this platform to say something; but it was also that I'd seen a sign at the bottom of the little path down to the towpath, an A4 handwritten thing about cuts to hospital beds, making the point that a decade of austerity had left the NHS ill-equipped to deal with something like a pandemic. I remember thinking, that's good, I'm glad people are putting things out – you don't see stuff like that anymore. I remember, walking to school as a kid, you'd always see bits of political graffiti around and it would sink in even if you didn't always understand what it meant. At least it gave a young person the idea you could make a contribution, an intervention politically, that there was such a thing as a public opposition people could be involved in that would reach an audience.

Then, yes, I thought, I'm in such a privileged position here on the towpath, on the busiest thoroughfare in the city during lockdown, everyone taking their daily exercise, I've got the whole side of the boat and if I put stuff here a lot of people will see it. I like the return to a more old-school kind of medium . . . a way out of the algorithmic tendency of the internet that pushes you deeper and deeper into your existing bubble, the way all these search engines generate stuff along the same lines you're already familiar with.

The vision he conjures up – of urban walkers, on their way to school or along the towpath, scanning walls and hoardings for political messages – takes me back to Solnit's words about posters:

> I have long thought of pedestrians, of people who walk their cities and know them, as keeping alive a confidence and familiarity that have great potential in crisis and revolution. These posters do for the walls what those walkers do for the streets: keep alive some power and some hope in the public sphere.

That hope is particularly hard to keep alive at a time when people are banned from public spaces and confined to their houses. Then the messages we do see – in windows, or on the side of a boat beside the river – have an added power and poignancy. But it's clear the side of a boat was never going to be a large enough space to contain everything this particular spokesman had to say.

I thought I'd like to push a little newsletter out of the boat, so I did that and left it on deck for people to take – here, have a copy – and I called it *The Daily Hustle*. I never actually intended to do one every day, but I thought I might do one once a month. I never got around to doing an edition two, so this is the only one so far. But in fact it wouldn't be bad timing to do another one. It triggered some interesting discussions.

The *Hustle* is printed on one sheet of A3 paper and folded in half. It has a three-part slogan on its masthead, echoing the three-point government edicts that became familiar during lockdown, but with a different twist:

Stay safe! Speak out! Resist!

On the front page is a statement from an anonymous contributor who works for the NHS, commenting on statements in the media about the over-representation of BAME people both among those catching and among those dying from the virus. It reminds me of what Darren told me at the lock.

It's taken a lot for me to not really explode until now. There is so much discourse right now re Black and Asian workers dying on the front line. I've seen takes such as 'Oh, Black people are more predisposed to hypertension, diabetes etc' as a way of explaining it. I'm here to tell you now what I call BS. The reason Black and Asian people are dying is a) lack of PPE and b) being thrust into the front line [. . .] There are numerous reports from Black health professionals who feel targeted to work in Covid-19 wards. Tell me why we will not die if we are overexposed and then have no PPE? This is criminal and it's glossed over by claps [for the NHS] and labels such as heroes completely minimising the issue.

We aren't f***ing heroes, we are human beings with families, loved ones and a majority of us are terrified because yes, colleagues are dying . . .

How did the editor of this broadsheet feel about the clapping for the NHS that went on, I asked.

I had these ambivalent, mixed feelings towards it. On the one hand I felt it was driven by something sincere and good on the part of people wanting to show their love and appreciation for those who were putting their lives at risk to tackle the pandemic; that was a thoroughly good and human impulse. But then over the weeks you saw it clearly being co-opted by the government as a way of deflecting criticism of what they were doing, through a show of patriotic unity behind people that their own policies were putting at risk and that was kind of distasteful, how it was used.

One of the main reasons we have the highest death toll in Europe is because the government has been determined to use Covid as an opportunity to ram through its privatisation of the NHS, so rather than implementing an effective test and trace system as other countries did early on, they've taken this as an opportunity to create a parallel, privatised health infrastructure, asking one company to do testing, another to take the test to the processing company and so on. It's been a disaster, and that's because these companies have nothing to do with health: they're security companies, accountancy companies. The government have gone out of their way to cut out public health officials, GPs and local authorities who are in the best position to run local contact tracing – until very recently they've not allowed them the data to do so and now they've reluctantly handed it over they've given them no funding to run it.

Very fraudulently they refer to their system as 'NHS Test and Trace' when it has nothing to do with the NHS. The NHS has become what Naomi Klein calls in her book *No Logo* an empty brand, in the way a huge company like Nike doesn't actually make anything, they put their brand on things made by others. In the same way the government are selling the brand of the NHS, hiring it out so these companies can use it to shield their operations from criticism and even make it unpatriotic to criticise them. The previous leader of the opposition was warning of exactly this kind of privatisation of the NHS and the prime minister was calling him a tinfoil-hat-wearing conspiracy theorist to suggest such a thing, but in the middle of a pandemic that has cost tens of thousands of lives it is exactly what they are doing!

It's clear from many of the conversations I've had, I say, that when we were clapping, many of us felt conflicted – we wanted to show our support but at the same time we were growing aware of the terrible problems health workers were facing. That was the problem with the action itself; there isn't really a nuanced way of clapping. If you clap, you are approving something!

Yes. I thought, what's the appropriate thing to do? Joining in you're getting co-opted, boycotting it means you're literally doing nothing, which is not very helpful, and at the same time I thought there was so much to be said that wasn't being said. I started going to different places each week and I'd do a little speech after the clap and it always went down very well.

There were very few opportunities to get out and about among the public during the lockdown – you can comment on social media or YouTube videos and so on, but the bubble nature of social media is well known. I had the urge to talk to people in real life and I thought the weekly clapping for the NHS was a fantastic opportunity: it was the one time during the week people were out in some kind of collective setting. The principles behind what I wanted to do were love, rage and respect really – I'd never interrupt the clapping, I'd make it very clear at the beginning that I felt it was right that we were showing our love and respect to the people who were taking such risks to keep us safe, but that there were also things that needed to be said. They were part of public sentiment and they needed to be expressed – the reaction I got seemed to suggest that was the case. Someone videoed one of the speeches, I'll send you the link!

He does and I see him on land, on the pavement at the corner of two streets; collar turned up against the chill, rocking from foot to foot, addressing those gathered outside their houses at the volume and with the emphatic gestures of a revivalist preacher, turning his head in both directions to broadcast words that carry across the still space with perfect clarity.

Please, brothers and sisters,
he implores as he draws to the end of his message,
we sent a message of love to our front-line workers,
and that's right,
– Hear, hear!
but please join me in sending a message of shame to this pitiless and shameful government and join me in saying
CRIMINAL GOVERNMENT!
– Criminal Government!
one or two voices respond.
BLOOD ON YOUR HANDS!
– Blood on your hands!
CRIMINAL GOVERNMENT!
– Criminal Government! (growing louder)
BLOOD ON YOUR HANDS!
– Blood – On – Your – Hands!

Applause breaks out, someone calls 'hear, hear' again before he concludes:

And please join me in a minute's silence for all those who have been unlawfully killed by these shameless and pitiless wretches who dare to call themselves our rulers . . .

And a silence does fall, perhaps partly in shock at the missile that has just landed in this suburban street, but mostly as a further act of solidarity added, by the arrival of this stranger among them, to their weekly ritual.

That looked like a powerful experience, I say the next time we speak.

There's something visceral and emotional in making a speech in a public setting, he replies,

and I realised after doing it that this is what freedom of speech means – not the freedom of the press or writing stuff, but speaking out publicly; this is a right we go on about but nobody really does it anymore. Nobody uses that freedom. You might have an organised demo where people who have specifically gone to the demo might listen to you, but just literally rocking up somewhere and loudly speaking out, that hardly ever happens. It really struck me that this freedom we supposedly hold as such a hallowed thing is so rarely used that, when it is, it is actually shocking.

One of the best things that happened was at one of the last streets I spoke on. An NHS hospital doctor came out of her house and said she normally stayed inside when the clapping was going on because she felt it was patronising and so on, but she heard this guy shouting and thought, what's this? It made my day, she told me, it made my day to hear what you were saying. Another guy on the same street was a care worker and he was also really boosted by it, you could see his eyes were lit up and he was quite buzzing from it. Care workers especially are treated as the lowest of the low, they get a secondary level of respect – NHS staff and oh yes, also care workers, a few weeks into the clap. They're mostly immigrants and as immigrants they are constantly demonised and humiliated in the press day after day, and for many of them their wages are below the minimum wage if you take into account all the unpaid travelling they do. They didn't get PPE for months . . . and so I think for this guy some recognition of what had been going on was empowering for him, and that was nice to witness.

You're hidden from view when you're inside the boat,

I say, but I'm sure you hear everything that goes on along the towpath, just feet away. Do you hear people discussing what's on the side of the boat?

Yes, I do. Sometimes I'll be inside and I'll hear people talking on the way back from the pub and then they'll stop and they'll start talking about my signs.

I remember one time there was a group of three or four Asian teenagers and I heard one of them say, yo, have you read this, and another one say, yeah, I've read it, yeah, and the first said, no, no, have you read *all* of it and the first one saying, oh, deep. I can't remember how it went on but I just liked the insistence that his friend read every last word.

Another time I heard these two young women say, ah, look at that, that's awesome, and so I stuck my head out and they were digging the signs and newsletters I had out at that time. It turned out one of them was researching the impact of Covid on BAME communities and told me about the failings of Test and Trace, so that was an example of me hearing a reaction and it leading to a fruitful conversation. I found that people who might not agree with the exact points I'm making still always welcome the fact that a public critique is being made – they seem to find it refreshing even when they might disagree with it, that there are opinions being stated that differ from the mainstream. I've never had anyone hostile to the fact that I put it out.

XIII

PARALLEL UNIVERSE

My own visits to a care home made me think about those with close family in such an institution during a pandemic, unable to give the support and comfort which every instinct told them they should to loved ones in the highest risk category for the virus. They must have experienced among the highest levels of stress and anxiety in the city. Nevertheless, when I found someone willing to talk with me about it, I don't think I was prepared for what I heard.

The care home his father resides in is located in a town that lies a few miles from the city. How long has he been a resident there, I ask?

He went into the home in October 2018,

he says,

so he'd been there for about eighteen months before the first lockdown. We'd had carers looking after him at home which was quite successful for about six months and then even they started getting a bit twitchy, because they felt it was too risky him being at home with his dementia. We did think about having him at our house, but his care needs are quite significant and none of us felt up to it, to be honest.

How did he adapt to his new life?

The care home looked after him really well, his physical condition improved hugely and he benefited from seeing a lot of people. The carers who work in the home are excellent and I really can't fault them. He just seemed much more cheerful; I visited him frequently and we could take him out for meals, to our house and so on, so we had all that freedom of movement.

Back in March we suspected there was already Covid in the home because everyone was coughing, but they didn't have any tests available to them. When you phoned up whoever answered the phone would be coughing, my father was coughing as well and I thought, hmmm, this is a bit weird . . . I was saying, do you not think he might possibly have Covid? And they were saying, no, no, he's just got a chest infection. I understand that that's what they were told to say because there was nothing they could do about it, no tests were available. The nearest tests the home was offered by Public Health England were a two-hour drive away, but if you go into the car park of a care home you will see that there aren't many cars there: a lot of people who work in care homes don't have cars, they're too poorly paid to afford to run them; so effectively nobody working in the home had access to testing at all.

Then one day I was rung up and was told that my father had had a fall, and he was just getting in the ambulance to go to hospital. The local hospital he was taken to was supposed to be Covid-free, so he was tested before he went in and they told me straight away he had tested positive. They took him in, established that nothing was broken and then they said they were going to send him back to the care home. That was the very same day the health secretary had been on television talking about how 'right from the start we have tried to throw a protective ring around our care homes' and that infected people would no longer be sent back into homes from hospital. I quoted that to the doctor – actually I spoke to two of them that day – and said, you're not allowed to do this, it's not right; we had, well, not exactly an argument, but a pretty heated discussion – and I remember this senior doctor said, I'm sorry, we know it's wrong but that's what we have to do. Those were his exact words.

And I'm thinking, surely that goes against the Hippocratic oath? By sending that person home you are knowingly infecting a community who are all vulnerable. So much pressure was put on the NHS to send infected people back into homes, that's what killed people. I had those conversations early in the evening and then around midnight, when I was in bed, I got another phone call and they said, we've changed our minds, just so you know your father's in an ambulance to the Covid ward in the main hospital.

Once he was admitted, of course, you wouldn't have been able to visit him. How was that for you?

It was a horrible time of not knowing what was happening, you just had the odd phone call each day with one of the consultants or one of the nurses and you just had to hope everything was going to be all right in the end. My father is as thin as a stick and everybody thought he was going to die from it because as far as we knew back then Covid was almost like a death sentence if you were quite frail. He was on the Covid ward for nine or ten days, he wasn't on a ventilator but he did receive a lot of other treatment. When he came back out the home was very good, they arranged phone calls and Skype calls and took it from there. They were doing their best under very difficult circumstances. Then when the first lockdown ended we were able to do garden visits. His room's on the ground floor and his mobility's not good so he was allowed to have a visitor as long as they were sitting outside his window. I just used to sit out there and talk to him through the window. He seemed to accept the situation – we had to remind him we're not allowed to do this or that because of the virus and he would say, 'Oh yeah.'

So when the hospital changed their mind and sent him to the ward, do you think he benefited from a change of policy that happened that same day?

No. Other people were sent back to the care home with Covid after that date, I know that for a fact.

So why wasn't he one of them?

Probably because I was arguing for ages, being a general pain in the arse! There were people in the home who died who were way fitter and healthier than my father, and I don't think they would have necessarily died if they'd had treatment in hospital the way he did. They would at least have had a fighting chance. GPs didn't go inside care homes during lockdown – my father didn't see a GP in person for months and months, it was all by video call. So these poor care workers, trying to help people who were dying in front of them, felt helpless and abandoned by the NHS because they didn't get the medical help that they felt they needed. All the care workers in my father's care home have been like people with PTSD; they're traumatised because they watched so many people die and they couldn't help them. All they could do was try and make them comfortable. Sorry,

he says,

and I hear the wobble in his voice,

I get very agitated when I talk about this! The only reason my father survived was because they thought he'd broken his wrist and he was taken into hospital. Otherwise he would have been in the home with Covid and suffered a similar death.

I suppose people will wonder how you can be sure there was Covid already in the home before your father went to hospital.

At least one resident in the home had a bad chest infection and went into hospital before my father did. It turned out he had Covid, but they still sent him back. They think that's how it spread among the residents. When you put your family member in a home you've got to have a leap of faith that people will look after them and do the right thing but during Covid the lines were very blurred . . . It became apparent pretty quickly you couldn't trust anyone.

So the policy was to keep you in the dark?

The staff regularly tell me they're not allowed to talk to relatives about what's going on – they're not allowed to discuss things like the deaths that have happened and that's very hard for them. This is partly due to confidentiality but also down to the fact that it's a business and they want to minimise any negative information around the business. If you can imagine, a lot of people have died in a short space of time in this home and the carers have looked after them for years in many cases, so they know them really well. But they aren't allowed to say how they're feeling, so at the time they were talking to us almost robotically, because they were mentally very much on the edge, suffering a lot, I'd say; seeing everything but not allowed to talk about it. They were visibly upset – it wasn't like these old people died peacefully, they died horribly, and it wasn't being acknowledged. They asked if there could be a memorial service for the people that had passed away, but it seems the management wouldn't allow that because if they did they would have to say how many people had actually died. Normally those lives would be celebrated, there'd be a proper funeral, but there wasn't anything like that. It sounds outrageous, doesn't it? It sounds like something I've made up, but it really isn't, it's for real.

That must have been appallingly difficult for the staff, not being able to talk about what they'd been through, but it must have been equally difficult for you, feeling you weren't being told the whole truth about the situation. How did you cope with that?

What I used to do, which probably sounds a bit weird, is go out there for a walk late at night and walk round the outside of the building to try and find out what was going on. Other relatives did this as well. We weren't allowed anywhere near the home at that point because of infection. Quite often there was just ambulance after ambulance pulling up, it was surreal. I felt so helpless because I couldn't get anywhere near him but it felt like if I just lurked around outside, I'd get a sense of what was happening.

When I talk to people whose relatives have died in care homes this year, I ask them if they think it was Covid and they say, we don't know, because they were never tested. There will be big clusters of people who died in care homes at that time and the government got away with brushing it under the carpet because there was no testing. It's been put down as chest infections or pneumonia and obviously old people do get these infections very easily, but to have big clusters like that dying in a short space of time is not normal. It's a huge scandal that infected patients were sent back into care homes and that's what the relatives of people who died – the Covid-19 Bereaved Families for Justice UK group – want the prime minister to address. They did a big projection on the Houses of Parliament of the faces of relatives of people who have died, asking for a meeting with the prime minister, something he had promised; but now he's refused because he knows there's been all these deaths and it's due to the policies his government put in place.

There is so much paranoia in those places. There are cameras everywhere. There's such a steep hierarchy, really. The people who work on the ground with the residents are very badly paid and their jobs are insecure and they are really undervalued, but they've all consistently worked all the way through.

How did it feel to have discovered what lay behind the official story of what was going on? Were you able to share it with others in the same situation?

I was going around talking to people about all these things and I think they thought I was insane. Unless you know someone who has had Covid or you've had a relative in hospital, you're not really affected in the same way . . . People I spoke to were thinking, what the hell, this can't be right – surely the government wouldn't behave like that, surely the hospitals wouldn't send somebody infected back into a care home; I even found it bizarre talking about it to people, because I could hardly believe what I was saying myself. It was like being in a parallel universe to everyone else.

XIV

BACK TO THE OLD WAY

September brings further change. Huddles of teenagers gather on corners in school uniforms that haven't seen the light of day since March: historical costumes from a period we scarcely remember. The streets are full of people once more, including crocodiles of masked and tentative tourists, aware the rites of the pilgrimage they are making may be rewritten overnight. In the city centre on an errand of some kind I cross a square frequented by coffee drinkers, drunks and the homeless as well as those with political and religious messages to deliver. Someone has set up a stand and a small group clusters around it.

END THE LOCKDOWNS

A slogan on the stand demands,

END SOCIAL DISTANCING

END TRACK AND TRACE

SAY NO TO THE MUZZLE

SAY NO TO VACCINATIONS

SCRAP THE NEW PRETEND LAWS

These are not sentiments I have seen expressed in windows on my travels through the city. A smaller sign at the side of the stand is positively gleeful in its rebellion:

IF YOU WERE MAD WHEN WE WOULDN'T
WEAR A FACE MASK, YOU'LL BE REALLY PISSED
WHEN WE REFUSE THE VACCINE!

A man in his mid-twenties with a neat beard and ponytail approaches me and holds out a leaflet, saying tentatively (he seems to have read some scepticism in my expression):

Controversial I know, but would you like to read this?

I take one with muttered thanks and stuff it in a pocket and the man appraises me for a moment then walks off. The truth is I know I should stay and find out what is driving these people, but for some reason I feel overcome with weariness. 'Say no to the muzzle'? Even though their number is small they seem to have used up all the oxygen in the square. Beside the stand an older, larger man with a white beard is display-ing his T-shirt to a couple of onlookers: it is designed around a visual pun, inserting an 'N' in red into the word Covid in white lettering, so that it reads 'Con'. It is provoking much laughter. It is quarter to three and I have a Zoom meeting at four; tomorrow we are making our third attempt at having a few days away and I'm keen to finish up work assignments and get ready. I decide to leave.

But as I cycle home the gathering in the square remains in my head. After a mile or so I stop and feel in my pocket for the leaflet, but it must have blown away en route. Of course, I should have spoken to them, what was I thinking? There is nothing for it but to turn back. Once again, I stand observing events in the square, struggling with my reluctance to initiate a discussion. Most passers-by, I notice, give the signs a brief glance and walk on. Some laugh or comment. A very few pause and engage. The drinkers, hunkered down on the steps of a monument, pass a bottle back and forth, apparently unconcerned. Then a suntanned woman in her thirties wearing a summer dress and holding a bunch of leaflets approaches me confidently, asking with a laugh:

You wanna talk about it? I've seen you hanging round, you're like, hmmmmm . . .

I'm just trying to work out what you're saying, I reply.

Not really trying to ram any sort of message down anyone's throat,

she says,

but I'm really interested in what people are thinking right now, because there's a lot of us who are thinking this has gone a bit nuts, a bit crazy. What's happening to our country? I'd love to have the facts and figures at my fingertips, but I think there was a report either from Oxford University or someone else who came out with a figure of 200,000 people will die as a result of lockdown. Because the government knows very well that if you plunge people into poverty it causes death. They've got actuaries, they can work this stuff out. Poverty equals death, mental health problems equal death, depression equals death – it's kind of like a death thing, lockdown.

So the strategy the government and the health authorities have followed to limit the virus is, in her and her friends' view, kind of like a death thing . . . I can see how coming to such an understanding would be an animating force – and she is very animated; in fact, she hardly draws breath, speaking for the most part with a broad smile on her face, yet with a certain toughness and determination, her stream of statements and questions interrupted by occasional bursts of laughter.

Social distancing is weird and unhealthy, it's against human nature,

she continues,

we want that to end – it's about having a discussion about it, really. Do we have to live like they're telling us to live now? I think everyone's under the impression it might end, but this is the new normal.

I notice you seem to have an issue with the idea of a vaccine, I say.

Yes, we're concerned about the vaccines, we want an open discussion about rolling out unlicensed vaccines. Is that what we want? Do we want to be put in a position where we can't work or travel internationally without having the vaccine?

So it's about personal liberty?

Absolutely! And is this the best way to fight the virus? Where is the scientific backing that says any of these measures have worked? The first lockdown is dead and gone now, but you have to analyse that and ask did it work?

I mention to her that in countries where the lockdown was enforced effectively – China, for instance, after their first phase of denial – they seem to have achieved remarkable results in reducing the death rate from Covid. She is not convinced.

They have to prove that. They should demand that of China. Anyway, is that what we want, that they model our society on China? Everything that China does, we do? That would have been unthinkable a year ago. We're living in a communist country here!

I want to tell her that it is unlikely she would be allowed to protest on the street about government policy during a national emergency with quite such ease in China, but another woman in her mid-twenties has come to the stand and picked up a microphone. Her voice booms around the square.

Good afternoon. As you might have gathered, we're here today questioning the official narrative regarding Covid. The measures that are being taken mean our lives have been affected in many different ways. The reason for all this – her voice rises a tone or two – is *supposed* to be that the government is concerned about our health. But if they're concerned about our health, would they be installing 5G on every corner and every lamp post? Because 5G disrupts immune system functions. I'd like to read you an educational poem . . .

And she begins:

> they call it the internet of things
> when it's installed we'll live like kings

but I can't focus on both voices at once and turn my attention back to the first woman, who hasn't stopped talking. So, I say when she pauses for a moment, are you also concerned about 5G technology?

Yes, 5G is an issue, they're putting in the 5G so that they can create this surveillance technology state for us, that's how we're going to live now, all hooked up to the smart grid and everything else, but have they asked us if we want it, have they done proper risk assessments, does it affect our health or doesn't it? People say this is a conspiracy theory but there are studies that say it's unsafe. Do we want to live in a smart grid surveillance prison? There's a failing in the media, there's a failing in Parliament, no one's having proper debates or discussion. This is why we're on the streets, you can't have this discussion on Facebook, or you get shut down.

There's no doubt the lockdown has had an effect on people's ability to protest – I've heard it again and again; there are views and emotions that can't be expressed in a poster in the window. On certain occasions, for instance after the death of George Floyd, the strength of feeling has broken down those boundaries and we have erupted out of our forced isolation. One door I knocked on in late August opened to reveal a couple I normally encounter out and about or at such events and who I had never visited at home. Activism and street protests are their lifeblood and they'd been busy organising and building new alliances during lockdown, but they'd also come up with a new form of protest, modelled for the times.

We started doing these cavalcades,

they told me.

So we'd get a group of us together in cars and we'd go to a particular place. Cavalcading is good – if you've got a PA system on the front car it's brilliant. We were bringing the message round about not going back to work until it was safe. When the two porters at the JR [hospital] died, we went around saying 'PPE for Health Workers Now'. It's a safer way of demonstrating. Lots of beeping and shouting . . .

Initially perhaps these two would assume they shared little ground with the woman in front of me, but she too has come up with her own way of expressing her views. If they were to meet and discuss what she calls crony capitalism – a phrase they would be completely comfortable with – perhaps they would find they had more in common than they first imagined. Slogans are complicated, the historian had told me; you can endorse a slogan coming from one side that you would repudiate coming from the other . . .

So, I ask her, you've had to come out on the streets because there is no other way to discuss these ideas? Back to the old way of protesting?

Yes, back to the old way . . . We just turn up in a town and I can't tell you how many people we get who come up and say, thank God that you're here, and they end up speaking to other people, because they're fed up, people are lonely. Because if they're the only one in their family and their friends who think this whole pandemic thing has gone too far, and they get ostracised, they've got no way to express how they feel. They can't express it on Facebook, you'd probably end up losing your job or losing your friends or losing your family, so they come and talk to us. That's it really, everybody gets their say.

They're doing, I realise, exactly what the boat-dwelling signwriter and the cavalcading political organisers have advocated – rocking up somewhere and exercising their right of free speech. The fact that much of what they say makes me uncomfortable is precisely the point.

Do you know anyone who's been affected directly by Covid, I ask?

No I don't,

she says.

People come along and rant at me 'my relative died of Covid' – fine, I never said Covid doesn't exist, but I'm sorry, you have to be dispassionate about these things, which is how a government should be, how the medical profession should be. When did we turn into such babies that we can't handle that some people will die? Why did we make this one illness the rock star of all illnesses, so that people who've got leukaemia, people who've got brain cancers are not getting treated? You can't see a GP anymore. What's going on? Why is my grandad seeing his GP in a tent in the car park? It's disgusting, it's dehumanising. People are having to send pictures of their private parts to their GP by email because their doctor will not see them in person!

I am distracted from what she is saying for a minute or so by a small drama unfolding behind her in the square. One of the drinkers has stood up and is crumbling and then scattering crisps from the large packet he is holding, instantly attracting a number of pigeons who swarm, their heads bobbing, around his feet. He walks towards the stand and they follow him, a grey, moving carpet, towards the space where the small demonstration is taking place. When he reaches a spot immediately in front of the stand he empties the packet on the ground and the air is filled with fluttering wings as a host more birds descend to join their fellows. Hey, what did you do that for, the ponytailed man protests, but the pigeons' benefactor merely closes his eyes to slits, leans forward and says, 'Fuck Off' in his face in a guttural growl, then walks back to his seat on the steps. All the aerial activity, combined with the unceasing stream of words the woman is uttering, unaware my attention has wandered, reminds me of the words of Francis Bacon: 'Suspicions among thoughts,' he wrote four hundred or so years ago, 'are like bats among birds, they ever fly by twilight.' Except during lockdown, he should have added, when world leaders are caught nightly on the news uttering all kinds of falsehoods, denying what is our daily experience, and we are forced to make up our own version of reality – in that situation, they fly as readily at midday as at dusk.

I glance at my watch: I'm running out of time, so decide to cut to the chase. You've told me what you don't believe in the official narrative, I say. So what do you think is really going on?

I'll explain my theory! The way I see it, this crazy crony-capitalism debt bubble has to burst sometime, OK? This is a controlled demolition of our economy, think of it like that. We are the economy, me and you, you doing your job, spending your money in my shop, but they don't care about that. What's happening during this controlled demolition to the big guys? What's happening to Amazon, what's happening to Google, to all the big players? All the billionaires have doubled and tripled their wealth. How many billionaires have you heard moaning about it? Me neither, that's what makes me suspicious. Whatever happens in an economic crash, the people with the money clean up, they do it every time. Then when everything goes tits up, we're on our knees which means we'll work for even less money, we'll be begging to get back to work and they won't have to pay us very much.

Whether you think there's a real pandemic or that they created a pandemic to bring this in doesn't matter, because that's what they're using it for, and this is why after the initial hype of the pandemic is over they're announcing they want to reset the global economy from the World Bank down. It's just accelerating all the plans they had already, getting rid of the cash, banking will be on your phone, everything will be digitised, what you have to ask in these situations is, who wins?

I can hear the bats fluttering louder, as she stands silent, staring me directly in the eye.

And now she comes to it, the driver of her fears.

I think it's chaos, they've developed chaos in order to build the new system up. Order out of chaos – as it's written on the dollar bill . . .

But I'm not a conspiracy theorist,

she says quickly with a laugh, acknowledging that this is exactly what she sounds like.

They don't care how many herd-class, livestock-class people die while the oligarchs come in to build up the new system. It's scary, it's coming out of my mouth, but I'm wondering, could this be a reality? That it's all going to collapse, and the shelves will be empty? Are we going to have to have a Covi-pass on our phone? You kind of see it already with people queueing to get into shops, you get into McDonald's and there's these scary announcements all the time, even in Sainsbury's there's all these announcements, keep your social distance, we're keeping you safe from the virus – what virus? We're all being made to behave like crazy germophobe hypochondriacs.

I'm interested in the possibility that certain ideas might be more prevalent in particular locations, so I ask where she has travelled from to take part in the demonstration today. To my surprise she mentions a remote location in south-west France: she has returned to England to visit her family before a threatened second lockdown makes such a journey impossible. Do you think, I ask her, that perhaps because you live in a very rural area . . .

She laughs again.

That I've gone crazy, you mean? I do sound a little bit crazy, don't I?

No, what I was going to ask is, do you think you're just not used to urban environments anymore, to the digitisation of contemporary life? That you might be in culture shock, coming back to the UK?

Oh yes, I'm definitely in culture shock,

she replies.

But do people know about their bodies and immune systems and vitamin C and vitamin D and zinc and all these things that ward off viruses? Are those things a conspiracy theory? I'm sorry, but if they say you can smoke your fags, you can eat McDonald's all day long, and if you wear your mask and wash your hands you won't get this virus, while all the time I have to walk around in a mask to protect you, I'm sorry, no – it's fresh air, exercise, clean water, clean food, clean air, that's how our bodies work. This really gets on my nerves, that people don't know how their bodies work. *You do not die of viruses if you are in good health!* That does not happen. Not really. The medical profession are utterly paralysed by the hype and the panic. And they didn't try hydroxychloroquine . . .

On this note it's time for me to go. I make my apologies, but I carry her voice with me, both recorded on my smartphone and in my head, where her unceasing dialogue continues to unfurl. Doubtless she will be posting about this event on Facebook, over the medium she so distrusts, to more followers than the small number standing around the edge of the square. This is one of the wonders of the internet – the way people previously isolated by the unusual ideas they hold can join hands across space, building global communities of power sufficient to disrupt the establishment agenda.

Or, as Darren puts it, when I tell him of my encounter: 'The squeaky wheel gets the grease.'

XV

IT'S MY FUTURE

On 22 April, during what we have come to know as the first lockdown, a poignant anniversary was observed: the fiftieth annual Earth Day, in which people worldwide would normally have been taking part in civil demonstrations demanding action on the environment, pollution and climate change. The first Earth Day, in America in 1970, saw 20 million Americans fill streets and parks across the nation in what has been claimed to be the largest civil action in history. Gaining support across the political spectrum, it seemed as though it had brought about a shift in global consciousness. Yet half a century on, the rainforests are burning, the icecaps melting and five new zoonotic diseases affecting human beings emerge every year as the result of our deeper and deeper incursions into the natural world.

How to mark the day, with schools, universities and workplaces closed and the population locked up at home? Many took part in online events, but many also put posters in their windows as a way of expressing their support. One window I notice has two artworks in it, one celebrating Earth Day and the other a more individual artistic expression I am keen to decode. The door is answered by a woman accompanied by her five-year-old son.

There were a lot of rainbows and teddy bears around here, she tells me, referring to other windows in her street.

We didn't ever really do rainbows and bears. Our window was a little differently focused. We did the 'Our Home, Our Planet' poster for Earth Day. These issues haven't gone away because of lockdown, they're more pressing than ever. The one in the top half of the window, I don't know if you can read it, it says 'Endangered Planet'.

It is as if the words plug the boy into a circuit and he becomes animated, eager to talk.

Well, I wanted to put that up so more people realise about the animals that are endangered,

he tells me.

– He made the poster entirely off his own bat,

his mother says proudly.

I examine the picture. It is clearly some sort of map, but its land masses are blue, in a reversal of cartographic convention, and the creatures that inhabit them remain mysterious to the untutored eye. Reflections in the window make it hard to photograph; when I look at the image later, his artwork floats in a wavy image of the houses on the other side of the road, as if reflected in water. So what animals do you have in the picture, I ask him.

I can't remember them all,

he says, suddenly deflated.

– We had different zones of the world, so up here's the Arctic,

his mother prompts.

– Polar bear!

says the boy.

– And this was the rainforest, over here I think, can you remember what the animals are, the one with the spots? He considers for a moment.

Black puma?

　— I think it might have been a jaguar,
his mother said.

Yes. Jaguar!

　— And then there was a monkey, can you remember . . .?
A red face?

　— A red-faced spider monkey. And then this . . .
Was a seal?

　— No, I think it was a giant otter.
Yes, otter.

　— And then over here we've got . . .?
He is jumping now.

Rockhopper penguin!

　— That's right, and up here?
Black puma!

A litany of names like a spell, each creature summoned up facing the threat of extinction, one of which, the giant otter (*Pteronura brasiliensis*), now confined to the Amazon, La Plata and Orinoco river systems, I confess I hadn't heard of before being informed by this young campaigner's poster. Imagine, a South American otter, six feet long! Another wonder, like so many others, that might have passed from the earth without my ever having been aware of its existence.

One thing that many observed during the spring and summer of 2020 was that they became aware of the natural world in a new way and found it a solace. Author Helen McDonald summed it up in a radio interview towards the end of summer in words which had me scrabbling for a notebook.

> The term apocalyptic is a really good one to use here, because in its earliest sense it didn't mean the end of things, it meant a revelation of things that have always been there but that we haven't noticed, and I think nature has worked like that

for many of us during lockdown. We're starting to notice things we haven't had time to look at before and they've been a huge comfort.

She's right: as well as the word's more usual meanings, which may be applicable for all we know to our world in the near future, the *Oxford Dictionary of the Bible* that my search brings up online confirms it 'means more generally an "unveiling" of divine secrets'.

An unveiling of secrets. The phrase sends me back to that notebook, in which I vaguely remembered I'd recorded an incident that though trivial in the normal run of things had seemed, in that hushed and brittle world, loaded with significance.

Encounter with a female blackbird on a path at the edge of the allotments. A breeze was blowing in the tops of the tall, slender birch trees that, when they are in leaf, obscure the block of flats behind them, always making me feel as I unlock the gate that I am leaving the city and entering a wood in Russia or Siberia, so noticeable is the change in atmosphere. The path ahead lay in dappled, shifting shade. I stopped. The bird had seen me but was so engaged with whatever it was picking up it continued in its task of tossing earth aside with rapid movements and rapidly pecking at the ground. I took a couple of steps towards it and stopped again. It lifted its head to look at me and I could almost hear it making the calculation, as it resumed its delirious feast, that it still had enough time to launch into flight if I came any closer. I remained still for one minute, two, then took one more slow and silent step before stopping again. Now it was quivering with tension, the sheer sensual joy provided by whatever it was eating in conflict with the primal threat

I represented. I was willing it to relax, move aside to let me go on my way, but when I moved again it was gone in a swift, direct flight down the path and into some trees. I examined its handiwork; it had picked through a mound of dry earth into an ants' nest and the orange insects were streaming out into the light. I picked up a stick and made the hole a little bigger, hoping to compensate the bird for the rude interruption to its feast if it returned, and I thought, what am I doing? I have places to go, things to do, deadlines to meet and I just spent five minutes standing on a path because I didn't want to make a blackbird fly away.

In my own defence it may well be through such moments of close observation that we gain a sense – however momentary – that we are sharing the planet with other species. And then as I write these words it hits me: the cognitive dissonance displayed by the blackbird, determined to carry on consuming despite the advance, ever closer, of something huge and terrifying, mirrors the current behaviour of the human race . . .

A few streets away a window bears two posters, a printed one carrying the Extinction Rebellion slogan 'We Want to Live' and a handmade green placard demanding that we 'Build Back Better'.

That sign was on my bike,

the woman who made it explains.

We (Extinction Rebellion) did a bike ride through the city; it was the first time we'd been back together since lockdown and it was very much about building back better. When I got back I put the sign in my window.

She's lived through the crisis in a busy house shared with two grown-up daughters, she tells me. I wondered if she'd felt closer to nature during lockdown, as so many others had.

Yes, I became acutely aware of nature; it was that wonderful weather and at the same time we had to be at home so I was initially in the garden all the time. I got an app on my phone so I could recognise bird calls; that was my lockdown learning! I'd been heavily involved with Extinction Rebellion, living and breathing it for around a year – I'd been arrested in October. I guess because of that I tune into nature a lot and lockdown made me do that even further. I went for walks – I never wear headphones when I walk because I want to hear nature, not mask it – and I found places to sit under trees where there wasn't anyone around, away from the busyness. I guess it was just more intense. It was wonderful not having planes going over and I remember just after lockdown ended seeing a vapour trail and feeling horrified. At the same time, I knew that other people were experiencing the crisis in a very different way – I was very lucky I was still working.

So yes, if there was a benefit to lockdown it was experiencing nature and thinking this really, really matters to me.

Not only to her. The young campaigner who lives in the next house I visit disdains posters in windows, instead chalking messages about impending actions on the pavement outside. She is thirteen years old, in year 9 at school and part of a group affiliated with the UKSCN (UK Student Climate Network) who carry out Youth Strikes one Friday a month – or at least they did until they were prevented from doing so during lockdown. What first inspired her to get involved, I asked.

Well, it's my future that the government is going to mess up by not acting,

she replies, in a quiet, dispassionate voice.

To change anything I need them to act right now and not carry on doing what they're doing, and so if no one else is going to get that to happen, I guess I'm just going to have to.

What form did the strikes take?

We would go and do die-ins outside various shops like Burger King or KFC or the bank. We would block the entrance to things, or we would all lie down on the floor in the street. Some people got annoyed and told us to move out the way, but most people were fairly OK, they asked what we were doing and stuff. We have massive banners.

You do these during school hours, don't you, I say. How does that work?

One Friday every month I would write to my head of year and ask whether I could leave school to do the strike, she says, as if it is a normal part of school routine.

We had to write a letter about why we wanted to go and why it was important to us. We left after the first period, so at ten o'clock. Normally we would be doing the strike from eleven until two.

So what happened when lockdown began?

We moved to doing digital strikes instead on Instagram and stuff. In the very first week of Covid we had a small strike, there were just a few of us on a Zoom call and it was mainly just to see each other, I guess, but then after that we had more people and we'd have a weekly theme that we'd research. One of the people in the group would send around a template with information about something and then we'd make street posters and send graphics to the Insta account and stuff. While we were on the call we would take photos of ourselves with our signs and put them on social media. Most people were slightly older than me. There's a bunch of people in my school who are about two years older and then there's people from other schools as well in the group. I'm not sure what schools they go to.

When street protests became impossible, did you feel these digital strikes filled the gap?

Well, kind of but not really,

she says,

because if you're striking on the street people will notice when they're walking past, but if you're striking online people who aren't actively looking for it won't notice it, and most people we need to listen to us wouldn't be actively looking for climate strike stuff. We've done one strike since lockdown, last Friday. We were striking in groups smaller than six and we split up and went around the city and there were definitely more people who noticed us than would have done online. We do need to go back to striking in person, I think, but now the rules are getting stricter again we don't want to do that if people are going to get ill.

As I listen, I grow increasingly impressed by the clarity of her vision, and aware of the great burden she and her friends carry. They know they cannot afford to leave their future in the hands of a generation that have demonstrated, beyond doubt, that they care nothing about it. At one point I ask if she's been inspired by Greta Thunberg and she just says yes in a bored voice. Old news, her tone implies. A new wave is breaking.

There's someone else, at the other end of life, who has done much to bring the danger the natural world is facing to the attention of a mass audience. A man who has spent his life on our screens, beginning as a youth recorded in black and white, tramping through distant jungles in colonial-era safari shirts and shorts, and now as an old man, in his nineties, clearly determined to spend his last years ensuring his message gets out. Generations of viewers have accompanied him on his travels, plunging from the highest mountains to ocean depths, marvelling at the variety of animal life to be found in the most remote locations. Secrets unveiled through a camera lens. Was it all just entertainment in the end? We are not used to such faces shown in unforgiving close-up on our screens: his hooded, mysterious eye; the new urgency that inflects a voice that, though grown a little hoarse, remains instantly recognisable. Somehow he now embodies the natural world he is speaking of, his demeanour reminding us of other creatures we have encountered on our screens: the immense weariness of the sole remaining example of a species of rhino for instance, its companions wiped out by poaching and habitat loss, as it lies down with a sigh in the dust; or the orangutan climbing the slender trunk of the last tall tree in an area of rainforest that has been burnt to the ground by loggers, from which it surveys the devastation that surrounds it with mournful gaze.

Apocalyptic times during which we have been given this brief moment for pause and reflection by a virus that, rather than being an isolated problem, is a symptom of far greater problems to come. Achille Mbembe writes:

> If, indeed, Covid-19 is the spectacular expression of the planetary impasse in which humanity finds itself today, then it is a matter of no less than reconstructing a habitable Earth to give all of us the breath of life. We must reclaim the lungs of our world with a view to forging new ground. Humankind and biosphere are one. Alone, humanity has no future. Are we capable of rediscovering that each of us belongs to the same species, that we have an indivisible bond with all life? Perhaps that is the question – the very last – before we draw our last dying breath.

I hesitate to ask the young campaigner *my* final question because I don't want to cause her any distress, but I need to hear her answer. I want to know how it feels for someone of her generation to have to think about these issues, to carry the weight of responsibility for the planet's survival on her shoulders.

It's really scary,

she says, for the first time allowing herself to display some emotion.

It's quite confusing as well. For instance, the information and the teaching resources about climate change they gave us at school were five years old, so they weren't really accurate anymore. The information from five years ago will be different from today and the statistics will be different. They don't – well, they do care, but they don't seem to as much as we want them to.

She pauses for a moment, frowns slightly.

At the very end of last year I was choosing my GCSE subjects, everybody was talking to me about what subjects I would be doing.

It's confusing to be asked to think about your future – when you're aware you probably won't have that long a future, if people continue doing what they're doing right now.

THE END OF THE BEGINNING

I am unlikely to die; I am certain to die. One statement true in the short term, one in the slightly longer. We come into this world wrapped in our winding sheet, as John Donne told us, seeking a grave. Yet somehow we must continue, even when the future is uncertain. It is my hope that the clues to how to do so – continue, that is – lie around us, in the present day. In the visionary wisdom of the young and the noble endurance of the old. In the courage of those who stepped up and made the ultimate sacrifice when their professional duty demanded it, as well as of those who took to the streets to challenge racial injustice and climate suicide. In the simple truths uttered on doorsteps, in pubs or on the floodlit floor of a Covid ward. In the lessons the birds and the sunset taught us when the throbbing engine of capital was, for a brief moment, stilled.

''Tis time to observe occurrences,' Sir Thomas Browne wrote in the dedication to *Urn Burial*, 'and let nothing remarkable escape us.'

Will the symbols of hope and resistance we raised in our dark hours sustain us through the next pandemic? Will we be ready to embark on another journey into the interior? One of the most eloquent signs I saw in a window during the first lockdown comprised just three words:

SEE YOU

SOON

How soon, we cannot tell.

Browne too lived in challenging times, in which, as he put it, 'the most industrious heads do find no easy work to erect a new Britannia.'

No easy work. But that, when the pandemic is finally tamed and the inquest over, is exactly what we'll be called on to do.

OXFORD, OCTOBER 2020

ACKNOWLEDGEMENTS

I want to thank all those who opened up to me at a time when circumstances encouraged us all to do the opposite: who were welcoming, in an appropriately socially distanced way and trusting enough to talk themselves, or let their children talk, to an unexpected stranger at their door. Most of those I have spoken to have chosen to remain anonymous, for reasons that will be obvious. You know who you are. To Alex Noble and Hasan Bamyani, thank you! Thanks too to Nicholas Cronk for pointing me towards the story of the Monument. Especial thanks to Stefan Tobler for having the confidence to set me on this journey and for the support he gave along the way. And to the one who carried on making connections when all the circuits were broken, the perfect companion and fellow-traveller through lockdown – this is for you.

SOURCES

Quotations from the following sources are gratefully acknowledged.

John Akomfrah, in conversation with Tina Campt, Ekow Eshun and Saidiya Hartman, recorded 18 June 2020, transcription at https://www.lissongallery.com/studio/john-akomfrah-tina-campt-saidiya-hartman, accessed 1 November 2020.

Francis Bacon, 'Of Suspicion', from *Essays or Counsels, Civil and Moral*.

Gilbert Baker, interviewed in Inside/Out, a MoMA blog, 17 June 2015, https://www.moma.org/explore/inside_out/2015/06/17/moma-acquires-the-rainbow-flag/, accessed 14 November 2020.

Hasan Bamyani, 'Darde Dell', translated collaboratively by Hasan Bamyani and James Attlee, first published online in *The Oxford Review*, May 2019: https://www.the-orb.org/post/darde-dell, accessed 14 November 2020.

Roland Barthes, *Camera Lucida*, translated by Richard Howard.

Sir Thomas Browne, *Urn Burial*.

Albert Camus, 'The Minotaur, or the Halt at Oran' in *Lyrical and Critical Essays*, edited by Philip Thody, translated by Ellen Conroy Kennedy.

Confucius, *The Sayings of Confucius*, translated by James R Ware.

159

Frantz Fanon, *Black Skin, White Masks*, translated by Richard Philcox.

Antonio Gramsci, *Selections from the Prison Notebooks*, edited and translated by Quintin Hoare and Geoffrey Nowell-Smith.

Claude Lévi-Strauss, *Tristes Tropiques*, translated by Doreen and John Weightman.

Achille Mbembe, 'The Universal Right to Breathe', originally published in French on the *AOC* magazine website, 6 April 2020, and translated by Carolyn Shread, published on *In the Moment*, a *Critical Inquiry* blog, 13 April 2020: https://critinq.wordpress.com/2020/04/13/the-universal-right-to-breathe/, accessed 14 November 2020.

Montaigne, *Essays*, translated by JM Cohen.

Cecil Rhodes, 'Confession of Faith'.

Rebecca Solnit, foreword to Josh MacPhee's *Celebrate People's History: The Poster Book of Resistance and Revolution*.

Olga Tokarczuk, *Flights*, translated by Jennifer Croft.

For information about shark migration and slavery, as well as a pointer towards the poem 'Summer' by James Thompson, I am indebted to the article 'History from below the water line: Sharks and the Atlantic slave trade' by historian Marcus Rediker in *Atlantic Studies* 5:2, August 2008, pp 285–297.

Two further poems by Hasan Bamyani can be found in *Crossing Lines: An Anthology of Immigrant Poetry* (Broken Sleep Books, 2021).

The exhibition *We Will Walk: Art and Resistance in the American South*, curated by Hannah Collins and Paul Goodwin, was shown at Turner Contemporary, Margate, 7 February–6 September 2020.

Dear readers,

As well as relying on bookshop sales, And Other Stories relies on subscriptions from people like you for many of our books, whose stories other publishers often consider too risky to take on.

Our subscribers don't just make the books physically happen. They also help us approach booksellers, because we can demonstrate that our books already have readers and fans. And they give us the security to publish in line with our values, which are collaborative, imaginative and 'shamelessly literary'.

All of our subscribers:

- receive a first-edition copy of each of the books they subscribe to
- are thanked by name at the end of our subscriber-supported books
- receive little extras from us by way of thank you, for example: postcards created by our authors

BECOME A SUBSCRIBER,
OR GIVE A SUBSCRIPTION TO A FRIEND

Visit andotherstories.org/subscriptions to help make our books happen. You can subscribe to books we're in the process of making. To purchase books we have already published, we urge you to support your local or favourite bookshop and order directly from them – the often unsung heroes of publishing.

OTHER WAYS TO GET INVOLVED

If you'd like to know about upcoming events and reading groups (our foreign-language reading groups help us choose books to publish, for example) you can:

- join our mailing list at: andotherstories.org
- follow us on Twitter: @andothertweets
- join us on Facebook: facebook.com/AndOtherStoriesBooks
- admire our books on Instagram: @andotherpics
- follow our blog: andotherstories.org/ampersand

This book was made possible thanks to the support of:

A Cudmore
Aaron McEnery
Aaron Schneider
Abel Gonzalez
Abigail Charlesworth
Abigail Howell
Abigail Walton
Ada Gokay
Adam Clarke
Adam Duncan
Adam Lenson
Adrian Astur Alvarez
Adrian Perez
Adriana Francisco
Aifric Campbell
Aisha McLean
Ajay Sharma
Alan Baldwin
Alan Hunter
Alan McMonagle
Alan Stoskopf
Alastair Gillespie
Alastair Whitson
Alecia Marshall
Aleksi Rennes
Alex Fleming
Alex Hoffman
Alex Lockwood
Alex Ramsey
Alexander Barbour
Alexander Bunin
Alexander Leggatt
Alexandra Citron
Alexandra Stewart
Alexandra Stewart

Alexandra Tilden
Alexandra Webb
Alfred Birnbaum
Alfred Tobler
Ali Ersahin
Ali Riley
Ali Smith
Ali Usman
Alice Morgan
Alice Radosh
Alice Shumate
Alice Smith
Alison Lock
Alison Winston
Aliya Rashid
Allison LaSorda
Alyse Ceirante
Alyssa Rinaldi
Alyssa Tauber
Amado Floresca
Amaia Gabantxo
Amanda
Amanda Geenen
Amanda Maria
    Izquierdo Gonzalez
Amanda Read
Amber Da
Amelia Lowe
Amine Hamadache
Amy and Jamie
Amy Benson
Amy Bessent
Amy Bojang
Anastasia Carver
Andrea Barlien

Andrea Brownstone
Andrea Reece
Andrew Kerr-Jarrett
Andrew Marston
Andrew McCallum
Andrew Ratomski
Andrew Rego
Andy Corsham
Andy Marshall
Aneesa Higgins
Angela Everitt
Angelica Ribichini
Anna Dowrick
Anna Finneran
Anna Hawthorne
Anna Milsom
Anna Zaranko
Anne Barnes
Anne Boileau Clarke
Anne Carus
Anne Craven
Anne Edyvean
Anne Frost
Anne Magnier-Redon
Anne O'Brien
Anne Ryden
Anne Sticksel
Anne Stokes
Annie McDermott
Anonymous
Anonymous
Anthony Alexander
Anthony Brown
Anthony Cotton
Anthony Quinn

Antonia Lloyd-
  Jones
Antonia Saske
Antony Osgood
Antony Pearce
Aoife Boyd
Archie Davies
Arthur John Rowles
Asako Serizawa
Ash Lazarus
Ashleigh Sutton
Ashley Cairns
Audrey Mash
Audrey Small
Aysha Powell
Barbara Bettsworth
Barbara Mellor
Barbara Robinson
Barbara Spicer
Barbara Wheatley
Barry John Fletcher
Barry Norton
Barry Watkinson
Bea Karol Burks
Ben Buchwald
Ben Schofield
Ben Thornton
Ben Walter
Benjamin Judge
Benjamin Pester
Bethan Kent
Beverley Thomas
Bhakti Gajjar
Bianca Duec
Bianca Jackson
Bianca Winter
Bill Fletcher

Birgitta Karlén
Bjørnar Djupevik
  Hagen
Blazej Jedras
Briallen Hopper
Brian Anderson
Brian Byrne
Brian Callaghan
Brian Smith
Brigita Ptackova
Brooke Williams
Burkhard Fehsenfeld
C P Hunter
Caitlin Halpern
Caitriona Lally
Cal Smith
Callie Steven
Cameron Adams
Camilla Imperiali
Campbell McEwan
Carl Emery
Carla Castanos
Carly Willis
Carole Burns
Carolina Pineiro
Caroline Jupp
Caroline Lodge
Caroline Perry
Caroline Smith
Caroline West
Carrie Allen
Catharine
  Braithwaite
Catherine Cleary
Catherine Lambert
Catherine Tolo
Catherine Williamson

Cathryn Siegal-
  Bergman
Cathy Sowell
Catie Kosinski
Catriona Gibbs
Cecilia Cerrini
Cecilia Rossi
Cecilia Uribe
Chantal Lyons
Chantal Wright
Charlene Huggins
Charles Dee Mitchell
Charles Fernyhough
Charles Kovach
Charles Raby
Charles Rowe
Charles Watson
Charlie Errock
Charlie Small
Charlotte Bruton
Charlotte Holtam
Charlotte Ryland
Charlotte Smith
Charlotte Whittle
Chelsey Johnson
Chenxin Jiang
Cherise Wolas
China Miéville
Chris Gostick
Chris Gribble
Chris Holmes
Chris Köpruner
Chris Lintott
Chris McCann
Chris Potts
Chris Stevenson
Chris Thornton

Christian Schuhmann
Christine Elliott
Christine Humphreys
Christine Stickler
Christopher Allen
Christopher Homfray
Christopher Jenkin
Christopher Smith
Christopher Stout
Ciara Ní Riain
Claire Hayward
Claire Potter
Claire Riley
Claire Smith
Claire Williams
Clarice Borges
Clarissa Pattern
Cliona Quigley
Colin Denyer
Colin Hewlett
Colin Matthews
Collin Brooke
Cornelia Svedman
Courtney Lilly
Craig Kennedy
Cynthia De La Torre
Cyrus Massoudi
Daisy Savage
Dale Wisely
Dan Martin
Daniel Arnold
Daniel Coxon
Daniel Gillespie
Daniel Hahn
Daniel Hester-Smith
Daniel Jones
Daniel Oudshoorn

Daniel Stewart
Daniel Venn
Daniela Steierberg
Darina Brejtrova
Dave Ashley
Dave Hill
Dave Lander
David Anderson
David Ball
David Coates
David Cowan
David Davies
David Greenlaw
David Gunnarsson
David Hebblethwaite
David Higgins
David Hodges
David Johnson-Davies
David Kinnaird
David Leverington
David F Long
David McIntyre
David Miller
David Miller
David and Lydia Pell
David Reid
David Richardson
David Shriver
David Smith
David Thornton
Dawn Bass
Dean Stokes
Dean Taucher
Deb Unferth
Debbie Pinfold
Deborah Banks
Declan Gardner

Declan O'Driscoll
Deirdre Nic
  Mhathuna
Delaina Haslam
Denis Larose
Denis Stillewagt &
  Anca Fronescu
Denise Bretländer
Denise Carstensen
Denton Djurasevich
Derek Taylor-
  Vrsalovich
Desiree Mason
Diana Baker Smith
Diana Digges
Dina Abdul-Wahab
Dinesh Prasad
Dirk Hanson
Dominic Nolan
Dominick Santa
  Cattarina
Dominique Brocard
Dorothy Bottrell
Doug Wallace
Drew Gummerson
Duncan Clubb
Duncan Macgregor
Duncan Marks
Dustin Hackfeld
Dustin Haviv
Dyanne Prinsen
E Rodgers
Earl James
Ebba Aquila
Ebba Tornérhielm
Ed Tronick
Ekaterina Beliakova

Elaine Juzl
Eleanor Maier
Elena Galindo
Elif Aganoglu
Elina Zicmane
Elisabeth Cook
Elizabeth Braswell
Elizabeth Cochrane
Elizabeth Coombes
Elizabeth Dillon
Elizabeth Draper
Elizabeth Franz
Elizabeth Leach
Elizabeth Seal
Ellen Beardsworth
Ellen Casey
Ellen Wilkinson
Ellie Goddard
Ellie Small
Emeline Morin
Emily Dixon
Emily Jang
Emily Walker
Emily Webber
Emily Williams
Emma Bielecki
Emma Coulson
Emma Dell
Emma Louise Grove
Emma Musty
Emma Page
Emma Post
Emma Reynolds
Emma Teale
Emma Turesson
Ena Lee
Eric Anderson

Eric Tucker
Erica Mason
Erin Cameron Allen
Erin Louttit
Esmée de Heer
Esther Donnelly
Etta Searle
Eugene O'Hare
Eunji Kim
Eva Mitchell
Eva Oddo
Ewan Tant
F Gary Knapp
Fawzia Kane
Fay Barrett
Faye Williams
Felix Valdivieso
Finbarr Farragher
Fiona Liddle
Fiona Quinn
Florian Duijsens
Fran Sanderson
Frances
    Christodoulou
Frances Thiessen
Frances Winfield
Francesca Rhydderch
Francis Mathias
François von Hurter
Frank van Orsouw
Frankie Mullin
Fred Nichols
Freddie Radford
Freya Killilea-Clark
Friederike Knabe
Gabriel Colnic
Gabriel and Mary de

Courcy Cooney
Gala Copley
Garan Holcombe
Gary Kavanagh
Gavin Collins
Gavin Smith
Gawain Espley
Gemma Bird
Genaro Palomo Jr
Genevieve Lewington
Geoff Fisher
Geoff Thrower
Geoffrey Cohen
Geoffrey Urland
George McCaig
George Stanbury
George Wilkinson
Georgia Panteli
Georgia Shomidie
Georgia Wall
Georgina Hildick-
    Smith
Georgina Norton
Geraldine Brodie
Gerry Craddock
Gill Boag-Munroe
Gillian Grant
Gillian Spencer
Gina Heathcote
Glen Bornais
Gordon Cameron
Gosia Pennar
Grace Cohen
Graham Blenkinsop
Graham R Foster
Graham Page
Gregory Philp

Hadil Balzan
Hamish Russell
Hannah Bucknell
Hannah Davies
Hannah Freeman
Hannah Harford-
    Wright
Hannah Jane
    Lownsbrough
Hannah Procter
Hannah Rapley
Hannah Vidmark
Hanora Bagnell
Hans Lazda
Harriet Stiles
Harry Plant
Haydon Spenceley
Hector Judd
Heidi Gilhooly
Helen Berry
Helen Brady
Helen Coombes
Helen Moor
Helen Wilson
Helena Buffery
Henrietta Dunsmuir
Henriette
    Magerstaedt
Henrike Laehnemann
Henry Bell
Henry Patino
Hilary Munro
Holly Barker
Holly Down
Howard Robinson
Hyoung-Won Park
I K E Lehvonen

Ian Hagues
Ian McMillan
Ian Mond
Ian Randall
Ida Grochowska
Ifer Moore
Ilona Abb
Ingunn Vallumroed
Iona Preston
Iona Stevens
Irene Mansfield
Irina Tzanova
Isabella Livorni
Isabella Weibrecht
Isabelle Schneider
Isobel Dixon
Isobel Foxford
J Drew Hancock-Teed
Jacinta Perez Gavilan
    Torres
Jack Brown
Jack Williams
Jacob Blizard
Jacqueline Haskell
Jacqueline Lademann
Jacqui Jackson
Jade Yiu
Jadie Lee
Jaelen Hartwin
Jake Baldwinson
James Attlee
James Avery
James Beck
James Crossley
James Cubbon
James Dahm
James Lehmann

James Leonard
James Lesniak
James Norman
James Portlock
James Scudamore
James Silvestro
James Ward
Jamie Cox
Jamie Mollart
Jamie Veitch
Jamie Walsh
Jan Hicks
Jane Anderton
Jane Dolman
Jane Fairweather
Jane Roberts
Jane Roberts
Jane Willborn
Jane Woollard
Janet Kofi-Tsekpo
Janne Støen
Jasmine Gideon
Jason Calloway
Jason Grunebaum
Jason Lever
Jason Timermanis
Jayne Watson
J C Blake
J E Crispin
Jeff Collins
Jeff Goguen
Jeffrey Coleman
Jeffrey Davies
Jen Calleja
Jenifer Logie
Jennifer Arnold
Jennifer Fisher

Jennifer Harvey
Jennifer Mills
Jennifer Watts
Jenny Barlow
Jenny Huth
Jenny Newton
Jeremy Koenig
Jeremy Wellens
Jess Hazlewood
Jesse Coleman
Jesse Hara
Jesse Thayre
Jessica Cooper
Jessica Kibler
Jessica Martin
Jessica Queree
Jessica Weetch
Jethro Soutar
Jill Oliver
Jo Cox
Jo Elliot
Joanna Luloff
Joanne Smith
Joao Pedro Bragatti
    Winckler
JoDee Brandon
Jodie Adams
Jody Kennedy
Joe Catling
Joe Huggins
Joel Swerdlow
Joelle Young
Johanna Eliasson
Johannes Menzel
Johannes Georg Zipp
John Bennett
John Berube

John Bogg
John Conway
John Down
John Gent
John Guyatt
John Hanson
John Hodgson
John Kelly
John Reid
John Royley
John Shaw
John Steigerwald
John Walsh
John Winkelman
John Wyatt
Jon Riches
Jon Talbot
Jonathan Blaney
Jonathan Fiedler
Jonathan Harris
Jonathan Huston
Jonathan Ruppin
Jonny Kiehlmann
Jordana Carlin
Jorid Martinsen
Jose Machado
Joseph Novak
Joseph Schreiber
Josephine Glöckner
Josh Calvo
Josh Sumner
Joshua Davis
Joshua McNamara
Joy Paul
Judith Gruet-Kaye
Judy Davies
Judy Lee-Fenton

Judy Tomlinson
Julia Rochester
Julia Sutton-Mattocks
Julia Von Dem
    Knesebeck
Julian Hemming
Julian Molina
Julie Greenwalt
Julie Hutchinson
Julie Winter
Juliet Birkbeck
Juliet Swann
Juraj Janik
Justine Sherwood
K Elkes
Kaarina Hollo
Kaelyn Davis
Kaja R Anker-Rasch
Kasper Haakansson
Kataline Lukacs
Katarzyna
    Bartoszynska
Kate Attwooll
Kate Beswick
Kate Gardner
Kate Procter
Kate Shires
Katharina Liehr
Katharine Freeman
Katharine Robbins
Katherine Mackinnon
Katherine Sotejeff-
    Wilson
Kathryn Edwards
Kathryn Oliver
Kathryn Williams
Kathy Gogarty

Katia Wengraf
Katie Brown
Katie Grant
Katie Kennedy
Katie Kline
Katie Smart
Katy Robinson
Katy West
Kayleigh Dray
Keith Walker
Kelly Mehring
Kelly Souza
Ken Barlow
Kennedy McCullough
Kenneth Blythe
Kenneth Michaels
Kent McKernan
Kerry Parke
Kieran Rollin
Kieron James
Kim McGowan
Kim Metcalf
Kim White
Kirsten Hey
Kirsty Doole
Kirsty Simpkins
K J Buckland
K L Ee
Klara Rešetič
Kris Ann Trimis
Kristen Tcherneshoff
Kristin Djuve
Krystale Tremblay-
   Moll
Krystine Phelps
Kyra Wilder
Kysanna Shawney

Lacy Wolfe
Lana Selby
Lara Vergnaud
Larry Wikoff
Laura Batatota
Laura Pugh
Laura Rangeley
Laura Zlatos
Lauren Schluneger
Laurence Laluyaux
Leah Zamesnik
Leanne Radojkovich
Lee Harbour
Leeanne Parker
Leelynn Brady
Leon Geis
Leona Iosifidou
Leonora Randall
Liliana Lobato
Lily Blacksell
Linda Jones
Lindsay Attree
Lindsay Brammer
Lindsey Ford
Lindsey Stuart
Linette Arthurton
   Bruno
Lisa Agostini
Lisa Barnard
Lisa Bean
Lisa Dillman
Lisa Fransson
Lisa Leahigh
Lisa Simpson
Lisa Tomlinson
Liz Clifford
Liz Ketch

Liz Starbuck Greer
Liz Wilding
Lorna Bleach
Lottie Smith
Louise Evans
Louise Greenberg
Louise Hoelscher
Louise Jolliffe
Louise Smith
Louise Whittaker
Luc Verstraete
Lucie Taylor
Lucile Lesage
Lucy Banks
Lucy Greaves
Lucy Moffatt
Ludmilla Jordanova
Luke Healey
Luke Loftiss
Luna Esmerode
Lydia Trethewey
Lynn Fung
Lynn Martin
Lynn Ross
M P Boardman
Maeve Lambe
Magdaline Rohweder
Maggie Humm
Maggie Kerkman
Maggie Livesey
Maggie Redway
Mags Lewis
Mahan L Ellison &
   K Ashley Dickson
Malgorzata Rokicka
Mandy Wight
Marcel Schlamowitz

Marco Medjimorec
Margaret Cushen
Margaret Jull Costa
Mari Troskie
Maria Ahnhem Farrar
Maria Lomunno
Maria Losada
Maria Quevedo
Maria Pia Tissot
Marie Cloutier
Marie Donnelly
Marijana Rimac
Marina Castledine
Marina Jones
Mario Sifuentez
Marisa Wilson
Mark Harris
Mark Huband
Mark Sargent
Mark Scott
Mark Sheets
Mark Sztyber
Mark Walsh
Mark Waters
Marlene Adkins
Martin Brown
Martin Price
Mary Angela
  Brevidoro
Mary Heiss
Mary Wang
Maryse Meijer
Mathias Ruthner
Mathieu Trudeau
Matt Davies
Matt Greene
Matt O'Connor

Matthew Adamson
Matthew Armstrong
Matthew Banash
Matthew Black
Matthew Francis
Matthew Gill
Matthew Lowe
Matthew Scott
Matthew Warshauer
Matthew Woodman
Maura Cheeks
Maureen Pritchard
Max Cairnduff
Max Longman
Maya Chung
Meaghan Delahunt
Meg Lovelock
Megan Holt
Megan Wittling
Melissa Beck
Melissa Quignon-
  Finch
Melissa Stogsdill
Melissa Wan
Melynda Nuss
Meredith Jones
Meryl Wingfield
Mia Khachidze
Michael Aguilar
Michael Bichko
Michael James
  Eastwood
Michael Friddle
Michael Gavin
Michael Kuhn
Michael Moran
Michael Pollak

Michael Roess
Michael Schneiderman
Miguel Head
Mildred Nicotera
Miles Smith-Morris
Miranda Gold
Moira Sweeney
Mollie Chandler
Moray Teale
Morgan Lyons
Moriah Haefner
Muireann Maguire
Myles Nolan
Myna Trustram
N Tsolak
Nan Craig
Nancy Jacobson
Nancy Oakes
Nancy Sosnow
Naomi Morauf
Natalie Ricks
Nathalie Atkinson
Nathalie Karagiannis
Nathan McNamara
Nathan Rowley
Nathan Weida
Neferti Tadiar
Nguyen Phan
Nicholas Brown
Nicholas Rutherford
Nicholas Smith
Nick Chapman
Nick James
Nick Love
Nick Nelson &
  Rachel Eley
Nick Sidwell

Nick Twemlow
Nicola Cook
Nicola Hart
Nicola Mira
Nicola Sandiford
Nicola Scott
Nicole Joy
Nicole Matteini
Nicoletta Asciuto
Nigel Fishburn
Niki Sammut
Nina Alexandersen
Nina de la Mer
Nina Nickerson
Niven Kumar
Nora Hart
Odilia Corneth
Olga Zilberbourg
Olivia Scott
Olivia Turon
Órla Ní Chuilleanáin
and Dónall
Ó Ceallaigh
Pamela Ritchie
Pamela Tao
Pat Bevins
Patrick Hawley
Patrick McGuinness
Paul Brackenridge
Paul Cray
Paul Jones
Paul Munday
Paul Myatt
Paul Scott
Paul Segal
Paul Thompson and
Gordon McArthur

Paul Wright
Paula Edwards
Pauline France
Pavlos Stavropoulos
Penelope Hewett
Brown
Peter Griffin
Peter Hudson
Peter McBain
Peter McCambridge
Peter Rowland
Peter Taplin
Peter Watson
Peter Wells
Peter Van de Maele
and Narina Dahms
Petra Stapp
Phil Bartlett
Philip Herbert
Philip Nulty
Philip Warren
Philip Williams
Philipp Jarke
Phillipa Clements
Phoebe Millerwhite
Pia Figge
Piet Van Bockstal
PRAH Foundation
Prakash Nayak
Rachael de Moravia
Rachael Williams
Rachel Andrews
Rachel Carter
Rachel Darnley-Smith
Rachel Dolan
Rachel Van Riel
Rachel Watkins

Ralph Cowling
Ramona Pulsford
Ranbir Sidhu
Raymond Manzo
Rebecca Braun
Rebecca Carter
Rebecca Micklewright
Rebecca Moss
Rebecca O'Reilly
Rebecca Rose
Rebecca Rosenthal
Rebecca Shaak
Renee Thomas
Rhiannon Armstrong
Rich Sutherland
Richard Catty
Richard Clark
Richard Dew
Richard Ellis
Richard Gwyn
Richard Mansell
Richard Padwick
Richard Priest
Richard Sanders
Richard Santos
Richard Shea
Richard Soundy
Richard White
Riley & Alyssa
Manning
Rishi Dastidar
Rita Kaar
Rita O'Brien
Robert Gillett
Robert Hamilton
Robert Hannah
Robert Sliman

Robert Wolff
Robin McLean
Robin Taylor
Rogelio Pardo
Roger Newton
Roger Ramsden
Rory Williamson
Ros Woolner
Rosalind May
Rosalind Ramsay
Rosanna Foster
Rose Crichton
Rose Pearce
Rosie Pinhorn
Ross MacIntyre
Roxanne O'Del Ablett
Royston Tester
Roz Simpson
Ruby Thiagarajan
Rupert Ziziros
Ruth Deyermond
Ruth Field
Ryan Day
S K Grout
S T Dabbagh
Sakshi Surana
Sally Baker
Sally Bramley
Sally Ellis
Sally Foreman
Sam Gordon
Sam Reese
Sam Southwood
Samuel Crosby
Sara Bea
Sara Cheraghlou
Sara Kittleson

Sara Sherwood
Sarah Arboleda
Sarah Blunden
Sarah Brewer
Sarah Elizabeth
Sarah Lucas
Sarah Manvel
Sarah Morton
Sarah Pybus
Sarah Roff
Sarah Spitz
Sarah Stevns
Sarah Wert
Scott Astrada
Scott Chiddister
Scott Henkle
Scott Russell
Sean Birnie
Sean McGivern
Serena Chang
Sez Kiss
Shane Horgan
Shannon Knapp
Sharon Dogar
Sharon McCammon
Shaun Whiteside
Shauna Gilligan
Sheryl Jermyn
Shira Lob
Shona Holmes
Sian Hannah
Sienna Kang
Simon Pitney
Simon Robertson
Siriol Hugh-Jones
Sonia McLintock
Sophia Wickham

Sophie Rees
Soren Murhart
Stacy Rodgers
Stefanie Schrank
Stefano Mula
Stephan Eggum
Stephanie Lacava
Stephanie Shields
Stephanie Smee
Stephen
    Eisenhammer
Stephen Pearsall
Steve Chapman
Steve Dearden
Steve James
Steve Raby
Steven & Gitte Evans
Steven Norton
Steven E Sanderson
Stu Hennigan
Stu Sherman
Stuart Grey
Stuart Phillips
Stuart Snelson
Stuart Wilkinson
Su Bonfanti
Sunny Payson
Susan Clegg
Susan Edsall
Susan Jaken
Susan Winter
Sydney Hutchinson
Sylvie Zannier-Betts
Tamara Larsen
Tania Hershman
Tara Pahari
Tara Roman

Tasmin Maitland
Teresa Werner
Teri Hoskin
Tess Cohen
Tessa Lang
The Mighty Douche
  Softball Team
Therese Oulton
Thom Cuell
Thom Keep
Thomas Fritz
Thomas Mitchell
Thomas Phipps
Thomas Rasmussen
Thomas Smith
Thomas van den Bout
Thomas Andrew
  White
Tiffany Lehr
Tim & Cynthia
Tim Kelly
Tim Scott
Tim Theroux
Tina Andrews

Tina Rotherham-
  Winqvist
Toby Halsey
Toby Ryan
Tom Darby
Tom Doyle
Tom Franklin
Tom Gray
Tom Stafford
Tom Whatmore
Tony Bastow
Tory Jeffay
Tracy Heuring
Tracy Northup
Trevor Wald
Val & Tom Flechtner
Val Challen
Valerie O'Riordan
Vanessa Dodd
Vanessa Fuller
Vanessa Heggie
Vanessa Nolan
Vanessa Rush
Veronica Barnsley

Victor Meadowcroft
Victoria Edgar
Victoria Eld
Victoria Goodbody
Victoria Huggins
Victoria Larroque
Vijay Pattisapu
Vikki O'Neill
Wendy Langridge
Wendy Olson
Will Herbert
Will Stolton
William Black
William Dennehy
William Franklin
William Mackenzie
William Schwartz
William Sitters
William Wood
Xanthe Rendall
Yana Ellis
Zachary Hope
Zachary Maricondia
Zoë Brasier

JAMES ATTLEE is the author of *Isolarion: A Different Oxford Journey*; *Guernica: Painting the End of the World*; *Station to Station*, shortlisted for the Stanford Dolman Travel Book of the Year 2017, and *Nocturne: A Journey in Search of Moonlight*, among other titles. His digital fiction *The Cartographer's Confession* won the 2017 New Media Writing Prize. He works as an editor, lecturer and publishing consultant and his journalism has appeared in many publications including *Tate Etc.*, *The Independent*, *Frieze* and the *London Review of Books*.